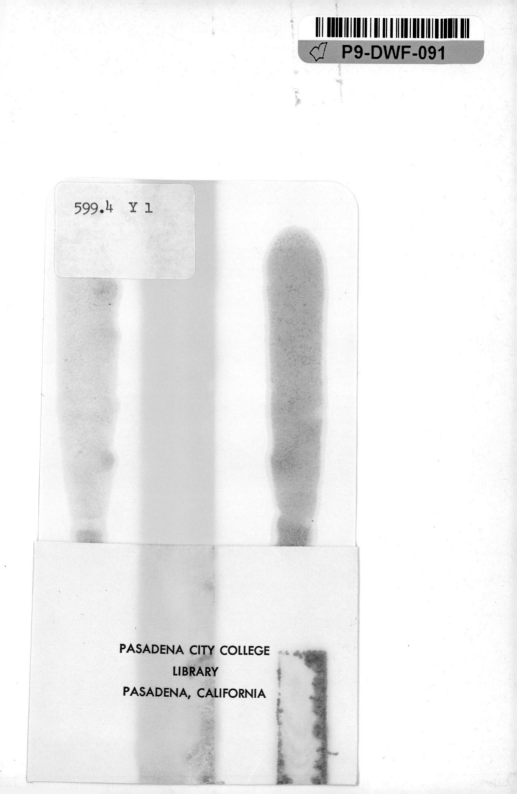

P9-DWF-091

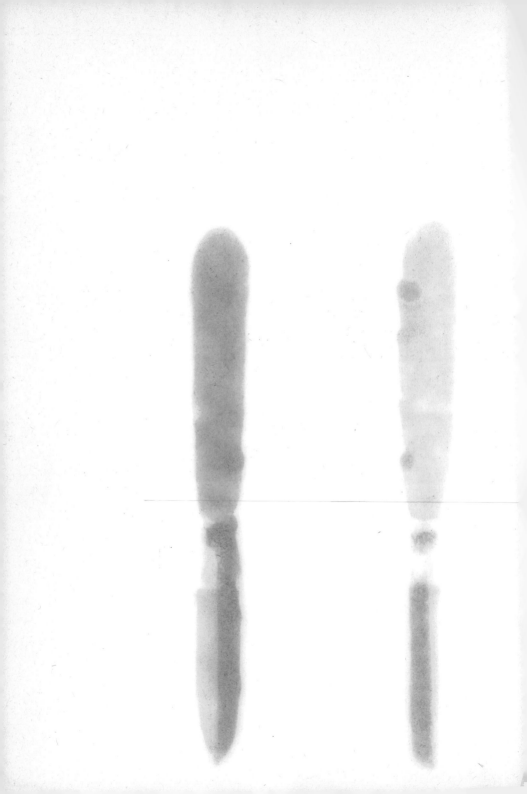

THE LIVES OF BATS

THE LIVES OF BATS

D. W. Yalden
P. A. Morris

A DEMETER PRESS BOOK

Quadrangle | The New York Times Book Co.

Library of Congress Catalog Card Number: 75-20692

Yalden, D. W. & Morris, P. A.
    The lives of Bats.

New York   Quadrangle/The New York Times Book Co.

76   6'25'75

ISBN 0-8129-0600-4

CONTENTS

LIST OF ILLUSTRATIONS

All photographs not otherwise acknowledged are from the authors' collection

INTRODUCTION

Of all the known species of mammal, one in five is a bat. Yet far from being familiar everyday animals bats remain creatures of mystery, the subject of more prejudice and misinformation than almost any other group of animals. They are instantly recognised yet poorly known, even to specialist biologists. Their ancient names of flittermouse and reremouse, the German *fledermaus* (fluttermouse) and the French *chauve-souris* (bald mouse) in fact only reflect a general tendency to label all small mammals as mice!

Bats do share with rodents such basic mammalian characteristics as hair, differentiated teeth and the production of milk and live young. However, they are immediately distinguished from all other creatures by their 'hand-wing', on the basis of which they are classified as a separate Order of Mammals—the Chiroptera (Greek Cheiros-hand, Pteros-wing). They are the only mammals capable of sustained flight, inviting the comparisons with birds which are made frequently in this book.

The relatively standardised body-form of bats makes their diversity of feeding methods all the more noteworthy (most eat insects, but many take fruits, nectar, pollen, small vertebrates, blood and even fish). Their physiological and behavioural modifications for hibernation, and especially their skills in flight and echolocation, are rivalled by few other animals and surpassed by none. Their role in the ecology of certain habitats and in the affairs of man are often of paramount importance.

The Chiroptera constitute one of the nineteen mammalian orders (others include Rodentia, Carnivora and Primates) and are themselves divided into two rather unequal suborders, the Megachiroptera and the Microchiroptera. The former comprises only one family (the Old World fruit bats or flying foxes) the latter includes all the remaining sixteen families of bats as in Table 1.

The ability to fly obviously gives the bats a considerable advantage over other terrestrial mammals when it comes to the invasion of new and distant lands (fig 1), and *Myotis* (family Vespertilionidae) has the distinction of being the most widespread naturally occurring mammalian genus (apart from Man).

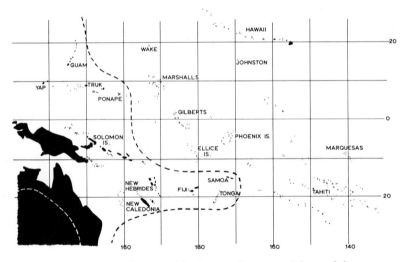

Fig 1.   The wings of bats enable them to disperse well beyond the natural range of earthbound mammals. In the Pacific, the fruit bats Pteropodidae (and members of other families, including Emballonuridae and Molossidae) have reached east as far as Samoa and the vespertilionid *Lasiurus* has spread west from America to Hawaii.

Even so, there is a major geographical division within the Chiroptera (see Table 1). Eight families are confined to the Old World, while six are found only in the Americas. Within each half of the world there is a large and thoroughly diversified bat fauna, but only three families have representatives in both hemispheres. Of these, the Molossidae have only one genus (*Tadarida*) in both and among the Emballonuridae the genera are all quite different in the two regions. Only the Vespertilionidae can be considered truly world-wide bats. There are many interesting comparisons to be made between the American bats and their ecological counterparts in the Old World.

TABLE 1

The families of bats and their occurrences in east and west hemispheres

		Approx. number of species	Old World	New World
Sub order Megachiroptera:				
Pteropodidae	Fruit bats or flying foxes	130	yes	no
Sub order Microchiroptera:				
Rhinopomatidae	Mouse-tailed bats	4	yes	no
Nycteridae	Slit-faced bats	10	yes	no
Megadermatidae	False vampires	5	yes	no
Rhinolophidae	Horseshoe bats	50	yes	no
Hipposideridae	Leaf-nosed bats	40	yes	no
Myzopodidae	Sucker-footed bats	1	yes	no
Mystacinidae	Short-tailed bats	1	yes	no
Noctilionidae	Fisherman bats	2	no	yes
Phyllostomidae	Spear-nosed bats	140	no	yes
Desmodontidae	Vampires	3	no	yes
Natalidae	Funnel-eared bats	6	no	yes
Furipteridae	Smoky bats	2	no	yes
Thyropteridae	Disc-winged bats	2	no	yes
Vèspertilionidae	'Ordinary' bats	275	yes	yes
Emballonuridae	Sheath-tailed bats	40	yes	yes
Molossidae	Free-tailed bats	80	yes	yes

Another fundamental feature of bat distribution is perhaps more evident from the maps in Chapter 9; the Chiroptera are primarily a tropical group and this has a bearing on many important

11

CHAPTER 1

THE STRUCTURE AND ORIGIN OF BATS

A bat's anatomy is basically like that of any other mammal, and the major differences all stem from a degeneration of normal mammalian features or (more often) their gross exaggeration. The wings are the obvious example, and at once distinguish bats from all other mammals. They are built of exactly the same bones as our hands, but the forearm and fingers are enormously elongated and the skin between them stretches out to the finger tips and back past the forearm to the knee or ankle (fig 2). Generally the fingers are about the same length as the forearm and can be neatly folded back alongside it so that the large wing is no impediment when crawling about. The free-tailed bats (Molossidae) have the longest fingers of all and an extra fold is needed to close their wings.

The hind limbs of a bat are also involved in supporting the wing membrane, but anatomically they are not nearly so specialised as the fore limbs. They tend to point sideways, sticking out horizontally rather than hanging below the animal. Lightly built and not very muscular, they bear little of the bat's weight if used for locomotion on the ground, though many bats are still able to scurry about in a very agile manner. The pelvis, though similar to that of other small mammals, is very small and weak. Some bats, such as the rhinolophids, normally hang up supported only by their hind feet. Their legs are directed backwards from the hips and cannot

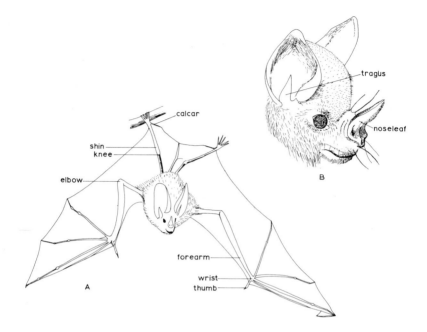

Fig 2. External features of a generalised bat, showing its basic anatomy. The close-up of the face shows nose leaf and tragus—not all bats have both.

be brought forward far enough to put the feet flat on the ground. An arrangement of the tendons ensures that so long as the bat is hanging by the feet its own weight causes the tendons to pull the toes into a tight grip and maintain their hold when the bat is asleep, or even after it has died.

The skull shows some special Chiropteran features, notably in the teeth (considered later) and the braincase. The cranium is often rather large in proportion to the size of the animal, mainly because of the extra development of the auditory regions of the brain. In some bats (especially Rhinolophidae) the tympanic

16

bulla covering the ear is enormous and seems to occupy a major part of the brain case.

Considering the number of species involved, bats are all remarkably similar in general body-form. Their most variable parts seem to be their two ends—faces and tails. Many bats have peculiar flaps of skin, constituting the noseleaf, on the muzzle; this serves to differentiate many species (fig 2), and some rhinolophids and hipposiderids have extraordinarily elaborate noseleaves. Other bats have fancy elaborations on the chin instead. The shape of the ear also varies. Most are simple, but in some (notably long-eared bats, *Plecotus*) the ear pinna can be almost as long as the bat's body, and may be folded away under the 'armpits' when the animal is resting. Within the opening of the ear, a small upright flap of skin forms the tragus. This—which is not present in all families of bats—may be tall and thin, short and crescentic, or some other shape which often gives a diagnostic clue to the bat's identity.

The tail can be very long and not included within the tail membrane (Rhinopomatidae), or absent altogether (many fruit bats). In most bats the tail runs down the middle of the membrane stretched between the two trailing hind legs and serves to support the membrane in flight. Some bats (Emballonuridae and Molossidae, aptly called sheath-tailed and free-tailed bats) have the tail moving freely in a pocket of skin, so that when the bat is not flying the membrane can slide up the tail, giving 'a bit more slack' to facilitate the use of the hind limbs in walking.

Bats are colour-blind and since they are mainly nocturnal, and frequent gloomy places, would have little use for the bright colours used among birds for display, courtship and a host of other social purposes. A glance through a collection of bat skins is therefore disappointing; they are mostly dull shades of brown and grey, with just a few white bellies to relieve the monotony. The few species with bold colours or markings are very striking: the spotted bat (*Euderma*), a piebald black and white species, is far more conspicuous among bats than a magpie is among birds! A few species of South American bats (*Uroderma, Vampyrops, Artibeus*) have a white stripe or two on the face and/or body, but these are often rather indistinct. Among African bats, *Lavia* has yellow wings; *Glauconycteris* species are boldly marked and have mesh-work patterns on the wings, perhaps helping to camouflage them among the foliage where they live, while hipposiderids (like *Hipposideros caffer*, illustrated on the dust jacket) occur as occasional bright orange varieties.

There is also usually little obvious difference between the sexes. Male microchiropterans are sometimes noticeably larger, and may (like *Otomops*) bear large and distinctive scent glands. Megachiroptera have good eyesight and sex differences are more pronounced; males are larger, brighter coloured and possess longer canine teeth. A few have additional adornments such as large throat pouches. Male *Epomophorus* have prominent tufts of white hair on the shoulders marking the position of well-developed glands, hence their vernacular name 'epauletted fruit bats'.

This uniformity extends to general shape and size. The smallest bats (eg Pipistrelles) are comparable in weight to shrews (about 5g); the largest bats (the 'flying foxes', Pteropodidae) are only about 1,200g, equivalent to a rabbit. These have a maximum wing-span of just over 1.5 metres (5ft), but most bats are much smaller, the majority weighing between 5 and 20g and having wing-spans in the region of 250–450mm (10–18in). Most of the other major orders of mammals achieve a much greater diversity of body size. All in all, the bats would be a boring lot were it not for the enormous interest of various aspects of their biology.

Throughout this book we are frequently drawn into making comparisons between bats and birds, and it is important to see these in perspective. Birds outnumber bats by ten to one in numbers of species (some 8,600 ranged in about 2,000 genera). Does this suggest that bats are biologically less successful? Certainly bats have a great diversity of behavioural and physiological abilities, but despite their wide-ranging feeding habits none is truly herbivorous (in the sense of eating grass or foliage as geese and

18

grouse do). None feeds like finches on dry seeds; none is truly oceanic, like shearwaters or even gulls; and there does not appear to be a bat scavenger (equivalent to the vultures), if we ignore old tales of bats eating hams (Allen, 1939). The large group of wading birds has no bat equivalent, nor are there any flightless bats.

From this brief survey it is obvious that many things which birds do but bats don't are in fact done by mammals of other kinds. A bat trying to adopt one of these modes of life would thus face double competition. To suggest from a direct numerical comparison that birds are more successful than bats is neither helpful nor valid. Bats are but a single Order of the Class Mammalia and as such are unequally ranked against the entire Class Aves (comprising 27 Orders), just because bats and birds share the ability to fly. Indeed we could turn the argument upside down and say that birds of no less than three Orders (swifts, swallows and nightjars) are, like bats, primarily adapted to catching insects in flight; yet together they total only 211 species, far fewer than the bats which hunt in this way. These three orders of birds achieve about the same degree of diversity (or lack of it) and are also similar to the bats in their size range.

THE ORIGIN OF BATS

Fossils of bats are rare and less than 27 genera of fossil bats have been described, compared with about 180 extant genera. This is a poorer fossil record than that for almost any other group of mammals. Even the rodents, which share with bats the characteristics of small size and taxonomic diversity, have about equal numbers of living and fossil genera, and for the horse there is a sequence of 24 fossil genera.

The paucity of fossil bats is perhaps partially due to their being inhabitants of tropical forests, where a host of scavengers, notably tiny soil organisms, swiftly consume corpses. Caves provide better opportunities for fossilisation, but though the bones of cavern-dwelling species are fairly numerous in cave sediments, such deposits are usually only recent (in geological terms). Caves in which bats were buried millions, not thousands, of years ago are rarely discovered, but one at Quercy in France yielded bats belonging to five of the modern families, dating back perhaps to late Eocene times, about 35 million years ago. The most advanced families (Vespertilionidae and Molossidae) seem to have been rare then, but more primitive ones (Megadermatidae and Emballonuridae) were common and the modern genus *Rhinolophus* was already present.

The earliest fruit bat does not occur until the Miocene of Africa (the oft-quoted Oligocene *Archaeopteropus* turns out to be a microchiropteran), but microchiropterans are present as Eocene fossils in both Europe and North America. Two middle-Eocene European genera (*Archaeonycteris* and *Palaeochiropteryx*) are represented by good specimens which show them to be quite obviously bats, though not referable to any modern family.

Currently the oldest bat known is *Icaronycteris* from early Eocene deposits in Wyoming, about 50 million years old (see fig 3). It lived 15 million years after the last dinosaurs had died out, and was flying around about 45 million years before the first ape-men walked the earth. Nevertheless it is clearly a fully formed bat and, despite its antiquity, does not serve as a 'missing link' between the bats and some older group. The elongated forearm and fingers obviously supported a wing. The ulna is reduced to a small splint of bone, fused to the much larger radius, as in other bats. The teeth are like those of insectivorous microchiropterans, though this bat does show certain primitive features (Jepsen, 1970) such as numerous teeth (38), more finger bones than most bats and the absence of a calcar. It also has certain features characteristic of the Megachiroptera, notably a claw on both the thumb and the second finger and relatively long nasal bones. So although *Icaronycteris* has links with both the modern sub-orders of bats, it is still a genuine bat and does not help us trace chiropteran ancestry any further back.

So how did bats evolve and from what group of mammals are

they derived? In the absence of fossil 'missing links', we can only speculate, using what we know of bat morphology and habits. A

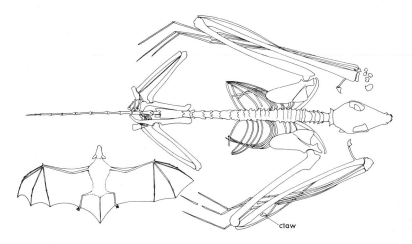

Fig 3. The earliest bat so far discovered is an almost complete fossil, named *Icaronycteris index*, from the early Eocene of Wyoming, therefore about 50 million years old. Basically, this is a microchiropteran, though it retains the claw on the second finger like many megachiropterans. The diagram shows the fossil as it is preserved and the sketch is an attempt to reconstruct at least the shape of the wings.

vital clue is provided by the basic similarity between the cheek teeth of bats and those of shrews and moles belonging to the Order Insectivora. Instead of the blunt cusps found on our own molars for example, the teeth of these animals have sharp pointed crests which serve to chop up the tough exo-skeletons of their invertebrate prey. It is reasonable to infer that bats may be derived from the more ancient insectivores, and certain other similarities of anatomical detail, for example the microstructure of their tooth enamel, support this. Both groups are mainly nocturnal and some shrews and tenrecs are believed to use a rudimentary form of echolocation. The fundamental dissimilarities between bats and all

21

other orders of mammals rule out most other possible alliances.

Although there are other groups of 'flying' mammals (eg flying squirrels and sugar gliders), these are herbivorous and not at all closely related to bats. Their 'flight' is limited to gliding down from a high point to a lower one; their motive force comes from gravity. Moreover, their gliding membranes are only an extension of the skin of forelimbs and flanks; they do not have webbing between the elongate fingers, as in bats. Only the cobego, or flying lemur (*Cynocephalus*), has a hand web comparable with that of bats, but this bizarre creature is unlikely to be a candidate for a bat's ancestor.

Still, suppose we imagine an arboreal *insectivore* whose gliding membranes incorporate the fingers (as in the cobego): unlike flying squirrels, it might be tempted to jump from its tree in pursuit of moths or other large insect prey, and parachute down to a lower perch. If the insect took evasive action our 'proto-bat' might be tempted to try and modify its own trajectory, and the finger webbing would provide an excellent means of varying its flight path. Natural selection could well favour more extensive webbing, to enhance manoeuvreability, leading perhaps to the characteristic hand-wing. If our hypothetical bat ancestor had been nocturnal, like other Insectivora, perhaps it would have had an additional incentive to develop its powers of echlocation, in order to detect and follow potential prey animals as they flew by. This line of speculation is at least a plausible one (just); and the first bats must have evolved somehow!

CHAPTER 2

FLIGHT AND FLIGHT ANATOMY

In order for a body to fly it must have an aerofoil surface (ie a wing), and the power to push it through the air. In aircraft these two functions are usually separated, with the wings firmly attached to the fuselage, and engines to provide the propulsion. In flying animals, bats, birds or insects, the wings are both the aerofoil and the propulsive system. Perhaps their nearest man-made analogues are helicopters, which use their main rotor both as the wing and for propulsion.

An aerofoil works because it is asymmetrical in cross-section; the upper surface is convex and thus longer than the lower one. Air flowing over the top of the wing has further to travel than that flowing underneath, so to reach the posterior edge at the same time it has to flow faster. In doing so it exerts less downward pressure on the top of the wing than the upward pressure of the air below. This pressure differential provides the lift that keeps the wing, and whatever it is attached to, airborne.

Notice however, that the aerofoil only works if there is air actually flowing over the wing, hence the need for a propulsive system. In moving through the air, some resistance (or drag) is encountered. It is physically impossible to produce lift without also producing some drag, but good aerofoils are shapes which maximise the amount of lift they produce while minimising the drag. Indeed, the lift-drag ratio (L/D) is used to measure the efficiency of aerofoils.

THE BAT'S WING

In bats the aerofoil surface is formed from a double membrane of skin, stretched from the side of the body and leg over four very elongated fingers. In many bats, the flight membrane, or patagium, also extends between the legs and incorporates the tail; a cartilaginous spur, the calcar, may project from the ankle, helping to support the tail membrane.

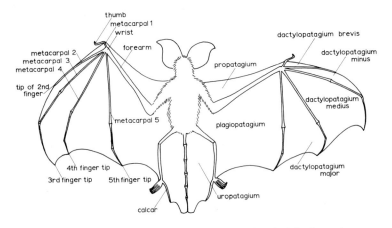

Fig 4.   The general structure of a bat's wings. On the left, the main supporting structures are labelled, on the right the different parts of the membrane.

The different parts of the patagium all have special names, which are useful in describing the anatomy (fig 4); the main divisions are the dactylopatagium (finger membrane—Greek *dactylos*, a finger), the plagiopatagium (arm membrane) and the uropatagium (tail membrane—*uros*, a tail). The membrane itself is very thin, perhaps only 0.03mm thick in small bats, and incorporates a number of fine blood vessels, numerous elastic fibres and also several small bundles of muscle fibres. There are about a dozen parallel muscle bundles lying wholly within the plagiopatagium, and a number of other small muscles which originate on the body and extend into the wing (fig 5). These muscles and the elastic fibres help to keep the flight membranes taut, though this is achieved mainly by skeletal elements and the muscles that operate them.

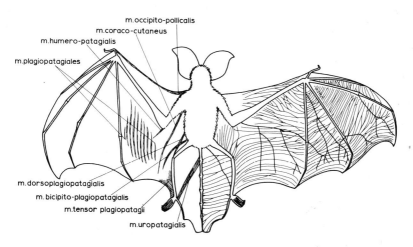

m.occipito-pollicalis
m.coraco-cutaneus
m.humero-patagialis
m.plagiopatagiales
m.dorsoplagiopatagialis
m.bicipito-plagiopatagialis
m.tensor plagiopatagii
m.uropatagialis

Fig 5.   The main support for the wing membrane is provided by the skeleton of the hand, but this is supplemented by a number of small muscles (shown on the left) and by an elastic fibre network (shown on the right). The heavier lines on the right show the courses of blood vessels. Not all bats have all the muscles shown—the uropatagialis for example is characteristic of Pteropodidae.

Digits two and three, together with the dactylopatagium minus between them, give the wing a fairly stiff leading edge. The third finger is the longest, and forms the wing tip; as well as an elongated metacarpal bone, it includes two or three phalanges. The second digit, lying ahead of it, is shorter, usually has two phalanges (three in pteropodids, one a claw), and is arched away from the third digit. A ligament runs from the second to the third digit,

25

while the extensor carpi radialis muscle inserts on the base of the second metacarpal. This muscle pulls forward (anteriorly) on the metacarpal, and the ligament transfers tension on the third digit, thus keeping this part of the wing stiff.

Nearer the body, the main strength is provided by the humerus and the radius (the ulna is very small, although in birds it is quite large), but the leading edge of the wing is a triangle of wing membrane, the propatagium, supported by a special muscle, the occipitopollicalis, running from the skull to the thumb. The thumb also projects forward from the leading edge and is usually referred to as a free digit. Although the two phalanges of the thumb *are* free (the end one bearing a claw used in climbing), the metacarpal may support the propatagium on one side, and a small dactylopagium brevis on the other despite being so short. Digits four and five support the main wing surface, the latter being particularly important because it is directed across the width of the wing (the chord) and can therefore control directly the camber of the wing.

One of the difficulties of designing an oscillating structure like a bat's wing is the inertia which is produced during each beat; it must be overcome in stopping the movement in one direction before starting the reverse movement. The problem is minimised by concentrating the weight of the structure near its pivot, as far as possible, which for a mammalian forelimb means keeping most of the muscles and the heaviest bones near the shoulder. Students of evolution are well aware of this principle as shown in the horse's limb, but it is equally well shown by the bat's wing. In the digits the metacarpal bones are fairly robust, but the phalanges taper off to very slender tips. The muscles responsible for extending the wing are mostly reduced to tendons, so that the wing opens automatically when the powerful flight muscles extend the shoulder. In the bat's hand, there are only nine muscles (eg in *Myotis*, Vaughan 1959) compared with nineteen in the human hand, and most of them are largely tendinous. The biggest is the abductor digiti quinti, running along the ventral surface of the fifth finger and controlling the camber of the wing. Even that muscle is reduced to a tendon in some bats.

Compared with the wing of a bird, this structure appears fragile and much less streamlined; it is usual for ornithologists, at least, to regard the bat's wing disparagingly. Actually, it is aerodynamically about as efficient as that of a bird; Pennycuick (1971) found that the lift-drag ratio of the fruit bat *Rousettus aegyptiacus* was, at 6.8, slightly better than that of a pigeon (6.0). This somewhat surprising result indicates a well-known aerodynamic principle: that smaller, slow-flying objects, like birds and bats, operate in a different scale of aerodynamics (technically, at a smaller Reynolds number), where streamlining is less important than in large objects such as aircraft. Indeed, as Norberg (1972) shows, it is probable that bats gain aerodynamic advantage by having their wing bones projecting above the surface of the membrane (fig 6).

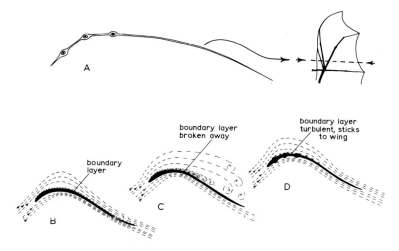

Fig 6.   A. The wing of a bat is highly cambered, in cross-section, but not very streamlined. The projecting fingers may be important in controlling the boundary layer, the thin layer of air next to the wing which is slowed down by friction. It should 'stick' to the wing surface, B, but in slow flight it may break away from the surface, C. One way of controlling this is to produce turbulence in the boundary layer (behind small projections D); the boundary layer then 'sticks'. (Based on Norberg, 1972.)

Compared with the tough feathers of a bird, the bat's wing membrane also seems fragile, yet the elastic fibres make it up to three times as resistant to puncturing as a rubber surgical glove, despite being less than one-fifth the thickness (Studier, 1972). Moreover, if it is damaged, the ability of the membrane to repair itself is remarkable. Church and Warren (1968) cut holes 2 centimetres square in the wings of captive fruit bats (*Eidolon helvum*) and found that they closed completely in 28 days, most of the closure taking place between 5 and 10 days. Davis & Doster (1972) obtained similar results with free-living pallid bats (*Antrozous*).

Indeed, a bird's wing may be more of a physiological disadvantage than that of a bat. Feathers are dead structures, so they tend to wear out, and they have to be replaced, usually once or twice a year; a 30g sparrow has to produce 1.7g of feather keratin to renew its flying surfaces. For birds in general this is a metabolic task arduous enough to be timed not to coincide with breeding (or migrating) seasons. The metabolism of a moulting chicken is raised 45 per cent, partly because of the rapid synthesis taking place as new feathers are produced, and also because its heat insulation is less effective as feathers are rapidly lost but only slowly replaced.

Of course, there are some real disadvantages in the structure of a bat's wing compared with that of a bird. For instance, Pennycuick (1971) found that while a pigeon could glide from 8 to 22 metres per second, the fruit bat *Rousettus* could only glide between 5 and 11 metres per second. The bird's fast-gliding ability depended upon being able to fold its wing, reducing the wingspan (from 70cm to 25cm), and this was only possible because the feathers closed over one another. The fruit bat was unable to reduce its wing-span by more than about 20 per cent (from 55cm to 46cm), because of the need to keep the wing membrane taut (fig 7). This necessity also means that the hind legs must help support the wings and this is a major drawback. By contrast the hind limbs of birds are not involved in the wing structure, and birds have been able to develop satisfactory methods of bipedal terrestrial locomotion.

The large surface area and naked skin of the bat's wing also mean that the loss of water and heat through it are likely to be high. This may be an advantage in flight, but could be a serious disadvantage at other times; for example, the wings could desiccate unless the bat chooses a humid hibernating site.

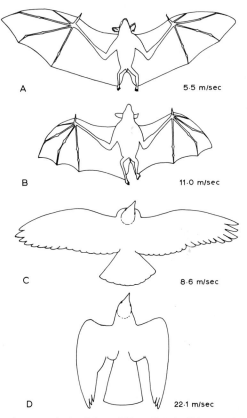

Fig 7. At slow speeds, both bats (A) and birds (C) spread their wings as much as possible. At faster speeds (B, D), they fold them back. Because the bat has to keep its membrane fairly taut, it cannot furl its wings so much as a bird, and cannot glide so fast. The bird is better off because its feathers can overlap and still form a functional wing even when partially folded (based on Pennycuick, 1971).

There are, of course, compensatory advantages. The musculature within the wing membrane, and the delicate adjustments which can be made by the fingers, allow a bat much finer control over its flying surfaces than a bird has. Contraction of the occipito-pollicalis muscle and lowering of the thumb produce a leading-edge flap to the wing, a well-known device to assist lift in aircraft; lowering the fifth digit increases the camber of the wing, again permitting very delicate control of the airflow. Moreover, the bat's hand retains much of its primitive mammalian ability to grasp food. Some insectivorous bats show all the deftness of a first slip in cricket, in making one-handed catches. Birds which catch insects in flight generally have to take food in their bills, though some use their feet. The bat's tail membrane can also be used in flight to catch prey, and as a pouch in which to hold food while it is dismembered and eaten.

FLIGHT MECHANISM

Basically, in bats as in birds, the wings describe a figure-of-eight path relative to the body during flight. During the downstroke the wing sweeps downwards and forwards until the wing-tips are well ahead of the plane of the bat's nose. The wings are, of course, fully extended during the downstroke, and the leading edge of the wing, particularly towards the wing tip, is tilted down (negative pitch). It therefore imparts a partial backwards force on the air, pushing the bat forwards. In the upstroke, the wings carry forward somewhat as they start to rise, but the elbows and wrists bend, so that the wings fold up, minimising the drag.

The extent of this folding varies according to the species of bat or, more probably, its flying speed, to judge from published photographs. The big brown bat, *Eptesicus fuscus* (in Vaughan 1970) does not fold its wings very much, probably because it is flying fast enough to get lift from the wings on the upstroke. On the other hand, the fruit bat *Rousettus* (Norberg 1972) folds its wings during the upstroke to the extent of producing almost a clenched fist, and the long-eared bat *Plecotus* turns its wings to a vertical position during the upstroke (Pennycuick 1972); these bats are almost certainly flying much more slowly than *Eptesicus*.

Norberg (1970) has also analysed hovering flight in *Plecotus*, where the wing-beat cycle is opened out from a figure of eight to a wide elipse. The body is held at an angle of about 30° nose-up from the horizontal, and during the downstroke the wings sweep forward more, but down less, than in level flight. In the upstroke, the wings turn vertically, as in level flight, but are then flicked backwards to give a forward propulsive force which cancels out the backwards force generated on the downstroke. This backward flick of the wings is also produced by pigeons when they take off. Hovering, at least in this bat, therefore differs somewhat from that of a humming-bird, which holds its body vertically and produces symmetrical forward and backward ('down' and 'up') wing strokes.

Despite the basic similarity of the wing stroke in birds and bats, the muscular and skeletal anatomy underlying the wing action is remarkably different. In birds only one big muscle, the pectoralis major, powers the downstroke; the equivalent pectoralis muscle of bats is one of four downstroke muscles, its action supplemented by the subscapularis, part of the serratus anterior, and the cleidodeltoideus (fig 8). Similarly, the upstroke, which in birds is powered just by the supracoracoideus muscles, is produced in bats by a number of muscles, including the rest of the deltoideus, the trapezius and rhomboideus groups, the infraspinatus and the supraspinatus.

Not only do bats use more flight muscles than birds, but these attach to different bones (fig 9). In birds, both the upstroke and downstroke muscles originate on the sternum and insert on the humerus. As a result, the sternum has a large keel (carina) which provides a large area of attachment for the flight muscles. The pectoralis major lies more superficially, and another function of the carina may be to prevent it from compressing the supracoracoideus beneath it, and perhaps interfering with its blood supply (in the bat the upstroke muscles lie dorsally, so the problem does not arise). The coracoid is a strong bone, bound to the ribcage and fairly immobile. The humerus has a prominent pectoral crest along its leading edge, to which the pectoralis muscle attaches, and also a notch on its dorsal surface into which the tendon from the supracoracoideus inserts.

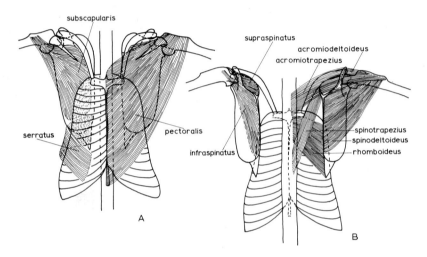

Fig 8. The main flight muscles of a bat. A—ventral view with the muscles responsible for the downstroke. B—dorsal view of the muscles responsible for the upstroke. In both, the more superficial muscles are drawn on the right and the deeper muscles on the left. A shows the bones in the 'up' position (ie prior to the downstroke), while B shows the 'down' position.

In bats, the pectoralis likewise originates mainly on the sternum and there may be a shallow keel or ridge developed, but this is never a prominent carina like that of birds (fig 10). Other parts of the pectoralis originate on the clavicles and the costal cartilages, and all insert on a deltopectoral crest on the humerus, comparable with the pectoral crest of birds. Other muscles run from the scapula to the humerus (infraspinatus, supraspinatus, deltoideus, subscapularis) or from the scapula to the ribcage and ver-

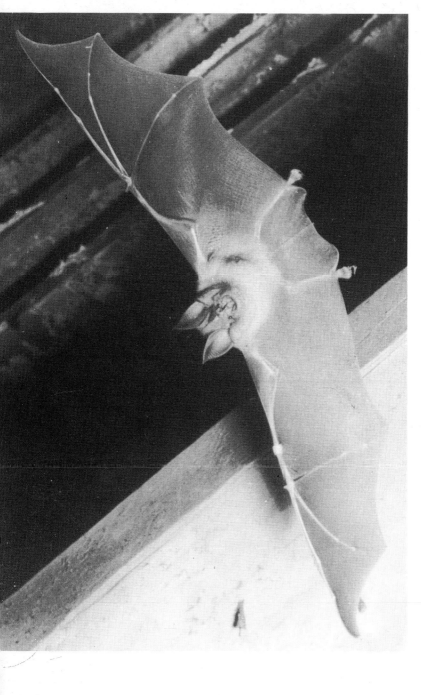

Page 33 Greater horseshoe bat in flight. The broad, low aspect-ratio wings are fully extended and permit highly manoeuvrable flight in confined spaces. Thumb, fingers (supporting the patagium), tail, calcar and noseleaf are all clearly visible. Bat is carrying a ring on its right forearm (Photo J. H. D. Hooper)

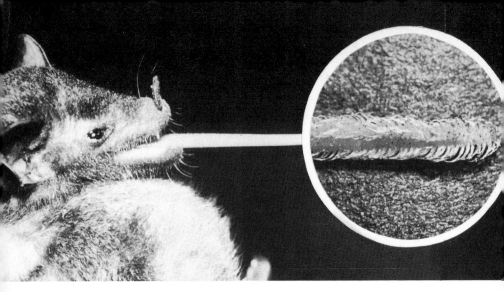

Page 34 (above) The long-nosed phyllostomid *Anoura geoffroyi* showing its long extensible tongue and the bristles at the tip (magnified) which help to pick up the nectar and pollen on which this bat feeds; *(below)* one of the extraordinary leaf-chinned bats, *Mormoops megalophylla* of the family Phyllostomidae. The fleshy elaborations of the chin seem to be the counterpart of the prominent noseleaf of other species, but their true function is obscure

tebrae (trapezius, rhomboideus, serratus anterior). The scapula then, is a much more important bone in the flight mechanism of bats. It is large, and instead of lying vertically against the side of the ribcage (as in most mammals) is placed horizontally across the back (as in man). The spine is well developed, as are the acromion and coracoid processes, and the blade itself is somewhat

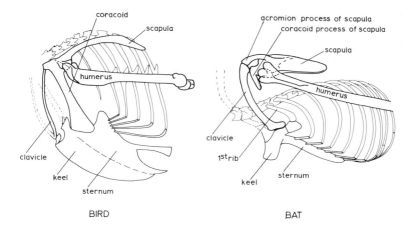

Fig 9.   The pectoral skeletons of bat and bird. The bird has strong coracoid bones bracing the shoulder joint and an enormous keel on the sternum. The bat's sternum is quite small and it is the clavicle which braces the shoulder joint. Note that it articulates with both the acromion process and the coracoid process of the scapula—in 'normal' mammals, it only articulates with the acromion.

ridged, all of which provide a greater surface area for muscle attachment. More important, whereas the bird scapula is rather immobile, the bat scapula rocks up and down, and slides across the back, as part of the wing-beat. The coracoid bone is reduced in all placental mammals to a small process on the scapula, and its role in birds of supporting the shoulder joint is taken over by the enlarged clavicles in bats.

In some bats (*Hipposideros, Natalus*) additional rigidity is given to the shoulder region by the fusing together of two thoracic vertebrae, plus the first two pairs of ribs and the front end of the sternum to form a solid bony pectoral ring. A further modification of

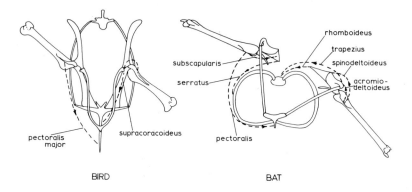

BIRD   BAT

Fig 10.   The lines of action of the flight muscles: downstroke muscles on the left, upstroke muscles on the right in each case. In the bird, both muscles originate on the sternum and the tendon of the supracoracoideus has to pass up through the foramen triosseum to get to the dorsal side. In the bat, many of the muscles originate on the scapula.

the shoulder joint in some families of bats (the 'more advanced' forms, particularly Molossidae) involves the development of processes on the head of the humerus and facets on the scapula, which combine to lock the two bones at certain points in the wing-beat cycle. These help to eliminate deviations from the most efficient flight movements and allow the different groups of muscles to work in succession without loss of power.

Bats are often regarded as underpowered when compared with birds, because their pectoralis muscles constitute only about 8 per cent of their body weight. In birds they can be anything between 6 per cent (grebes) and 33 per cent (some doves) of the body weight, but average about 16 per cent. This comparison overlooks the other downstroke muscles in bats; the four pairs of muscles together account for about 12 per cent of the body weight. This is a much more respectable figure, and is moreover about the same proportion that the pectoralis majors form in many small birds of comparable habits, such as warblers, flycatchers, and some swallows.

The major differences in design between birds and bats may partly reflect different ancestry; in the reptilian ancestors of birds, the ventral part of the pectoral girdle, the coracoid, was a large bone and attached to the sternum. Since the scapula and coracoid between them provide the articular cup for the head of the humerus, it was perhaps inevitable that they should remain fairly immobile in birds and provide a firm base on which the humerus could pivot. In mammals, on the other hand, the coracoid is reduced, leaving the scapula alone to articulate with the humerus and also leaving it free to swing on the ribcage. Even a horse uses its serratus and rhomboideus muscles to swing its scapula during running, and it is not so surprising that bats should exploit this same mobility. There may also be advantages. For instance, bat flight is exceedingly manoeuvrable and the involvement of so many muscles in flight may enhance the level of control. A bird, presumably, only has the choice of contracting the pectoralis majors or not doing so. The habit of many bats of roosting in narrow crevices may be one which was basic to the order. A shallow body is obviously advantageous here; the deep chest of a bird, a result of its large keeled sternum, is incompatible with this habit.

FLIGHT PHYSIOLOGY

Flight is of course a very energetic activity, but before 1969 very little was known about this aspect of bat biology. Recently *Phyllostomus hastatus*, a fairly large (100g) species, was persuaded to fly in captivity carrying instruments to record pulse rate and wearing an 'oxygen' mask so that energy expenditure could be calculated (Thomas and Suthers, 1972; Suthers, Thomas and Suthers, 1972).

The major problem during heavy exercise for any animal is

obtaining sufficient oxygen and transporting it to the muscles where it is required. For the *Phyllostomus*, oxygen consumption increased from 7ml of oxygen per gramme body weight per hour when resting, to 27ml in flight. To achieve such an increase, the rates of heart-beat and respiration can be increased, in an individual responding to each bout of exercise, and in evolutionary terms the oxygen-carrying capacity of the blood and relative size of the heart can also be stepped up. The muscles may also endure an oxygen debt during the period of exercise, which is repaid later. Bats appear to do all these things to varying degrees. In an individual bat the pulse rate may increase from 522 beats per minute when at rest to 822 per minute in flight, and the breathing rate from 180 to 576 per minute. These levels of change are comparable with those seen in flying birds.

The heart in bats is bigger than that of terrestrial mammals, about 0.9 per cent of the body weight compared with 0.5 per cent, so that more blood is pumped round the body at each beat. Birds have proportionately even bigger hearts, 1.5 per cent of their total body-weight. In bats oxygen-carrying capacity of the blood is 27 volumes per cent, much higher than that of birds (19–20 volumes per cent) or terrestrial mammals (18 volumes per cent).

Since the efficiency of oxygen exchange in the lungs is comparable in bats and birds, it seems that bats compensate for their slightly smaller hearts by the better oxygen-carrying capacity of their blood. The accumulated oxygen deficit in the bats' tissues, as measured by the lactic-acid concentration of the blood, does increase during flight, but the values reached are comparable to those seen in exercising rats and mice, and are to be regarded as a result of muscular activity rather than an adaptation to flight. Similarly, the body temperature rises to 41.8°C and then stays steady. As the body temperature rises, so the tiny blood vessels in the wings dilate, and form a particularly effective radiator during flight because of the cooling effect of the air stream.

Suthers found in *Phyllostomus* that the respiratory cycle in flight was linked to the wing-beat cycle, both occurring at about 10 cycles per second. A similar link is found in some birds, notably in the pigeon, but in smaller birds the correspondence is not maintained and it may also be independent in smaller bats. There is, however, a remarkable difference in the relative timing of the two cycles, even between *Phyllostomus* and the pigeon. The bird breathes in during the upstroke; expiration coincides with the downbeat of the wings and is maximal when the wings are at the bottom of the downstroke. Presumably, the pectoralis major not only pulls the humerus down, but also compresses the thorax. One might expect a similar situation in the bat, but here inspiration occurs during the downstroke and expiration during the upstroke. The ribcage is fairly rigid in bats, and the diaphragm and sides of the abdominal wall seem to be responsible for respiratory activity.

One odd result obtained by Thomas and Suthers was that the respiratory quotient* of their *Phyllostomus* in flight was approximately 1.0; an indication that the bat was using carbohydrate as fuel. Migrating birds use fat as their energy source, since 1g of fat yields about eight times as much energy as the same weight of carbohydrate, and their respiratory quotient is about 0.7. Pigeons are known to start flying using carbohydrate and then switch to fat metabolism, and dogs show a similar switch in metabolism during heavy exercise. Probably migratory bats will be found to have fat-based metabolism in sustained flight.

This peculiarity and the details of Suthers' observations should be interpreted cautiously, since *Phyllostomus* is a large bat, perhaps behaving a little abnormally in trying to control its flight under experimental conditions; it was also carrying apparatus totalling over 10 per cent of its own body weight and its calculated lift/drag ratio was only 2.5. More important, the species only flies for short periods ($4\frac{1}{2}$ minutes in the experiments perhaps 10 minutes in the wild), and bats flying for longer periods may differ in their physiology.

* Respiratory quotient: ratio of volume of carbon. dioxide breathed out to volume of oxygen breathed in.

DESIGNS FOR STYLES OF FLIGHT

The amount of lift (L) produced by an aircraft depends primarily on the airspeed (V), the wing area (S), and the coefficient of lift (CL).* This is a dimensionless number, and is an index of the aerodynamic efficiency of the particular aerofoil. In practice, a bat (or an aircraft) can therefore alter the amount of lift it needs (eg to climb or dive) by altering any of these factors. Conversely, any change in one or all of these will automatically change the amount of lift which is produced. As we have seen, bats are probably best at changing the coefficient of lift by altering the camber of their wings.

Similar reasoning applies when one considers bats of different habits. A bat which habitually flies fast (ie with a high value for V) needs less wing area (S) to produce enough lift to keep itself up than does one of the same weight which normally flies more slowly. Indeed, we can turn this argument round the other way, because drag varies in accordance with a similar formula.† Not only does a fast-flying bat *need* less wing area, but it gains the advantage (by reducing its wing area) of reducing its drag. Conversely, of course, slow-flying bats, particularly ones which carry large loads of food back to a roost, as some fruit bats do, will want to produce as much lift as possible, and have a relatively large wing area.

The extent to which such reasoning actually applies to bats is indicated by the figures for wing-loading, which is simply the weight carried per unit of wing area:

$$\frac{\text{weight}}{\text{wing area}} \left(\frac{W}{S} \right),$$

and is usually quoted in grammes per square centimetre (Newtons per square centimetre would be more correct). Unfortunately, there is a major complication to a simple comparison

* $L = C_L \frac{1}{2} \rho V^2 S$, where ρ = air density.

† $D = C_D \frac{1}{2} \rho V^2 S$, where D = Drag, C_D = coefficient of drag.

of wing-loadings between different species: size itself also affects wing-loading. Weight is proportional to volume and therefore to the cube of length; wing area, on the other hand, is proportional to the square of length. Wing-loading, therefore, is proportional to length.* In other words, a bigger bat is likely to have a higher wing-loading than a smaller one, irrespective of whether it flies faster; indeed, because it has a higher wing-loading, it *has* to fly faster to produce enough lift, or have proportionately enormous wings.

The figures in table 2 show this effect. The biggest species, the fruit bats *Pteropus* and *Eidolon*, have much higher wing-loadings

TABLE 2

Aerodynamic properties of wings of selected bats and birds. Data arranged in order of increasing body size, based on Greenewalt (1962) and Farney & Fleharty (1969). Birds achieve much higher weights, wing-loadings and aspect-ratios than bats; but within the common size range, bats usually have lower wing-loadings but higher aspect-ratios.

BATS	*Weight* gm	*Wing-loading* gm/cm²	*Aspect ratio*
Pipistrellus hesperus (V)	4·4	0·07	6·4
Myotis veli fer (V)	9·1	0·06	6·7
Tadarida brasiliensis (M)	12·5	0·11	8·6
Lasiurus cinereus (V)	27·0	0·13	8·3
Artibeus jamaicensis (P)	45·0	0·22	5·6
Eumops perotis (M)	55·0	0·27	10·0
Pteropus vampyrus (Pt)	1,380·0	0·85	8·8

V = Vespertilionid; M = Molossid; P = Phyllostomid; Pt = Pteropodid

BIRDS			
Regulus regulus (goldcrest)	3·8	0·12	6·4
Dendroica petechia (warbler)	8·8	0·13	4·9
Passer domesticus (sparrow)	30·0	0·30	6·3
Apus apus (swift)	36·2	0·22	10·7
Alca torda (auk)	780·0	2·00	12·1
Aquila chrysaetus (eagle)	3,712·0	0·69	8·4
Diomedea exulans (albatross)	8,502·0	1·40	18·7

* Algebraically, $W \, a \, L^3 : S \, a \, L^2 : \dfrac{W}{S} \, a \, \dfrac{L^3}{L^2} \, a \, L$

than any of the smaller, insectivorous, species. The very large birds show this in even more extreme form, with both sizes and wing-loadings far above those of bats.

Yet the effect of speed on reducing necessary wing area and therefore increasing wing-loading is also evident. For example *Tadarida brasiliensis* and *Myotis velifer* are about the same size, with wing-spans of 300mm; but the *Tadarida*, a fast-flying molossid, has a wing-loading almost twice that of the *Myotis*. *Eumops* is another molossid, of almost the same hunting habits as a swift, and it is interesting to find that they have similar wing-loadings. The table also shows that bats tend to have lower wing-loadings than birds of comparable sizes; this is probably another example of the effect of speed on wing-loading, because bats, by and large, fly more slowly than birds.

The aspect-ratio gives a second useful indicator of flying ability. Aspect ratio is defined very simply as the wingspan divided by the mean chord (the average width of the wing, leading edge to trailing edge).

In practice, it is not very easy to measure the chord on irregular-shaped wings, and an alternative way of expressing the aspect-ratio is the wingspan squared divided by the wing area. A wing of high aspect-ratio is a 'long thin' wing, like that of a sailplane, while a low aspect-ratio wing is a 'short broad' one, like that of a vulture.

Because of the pressure difference between the lower and upper surface of a wing, air tends to flow up round the wingtip, with a consequent reduction of lift. This loss is greater on a wing of low aspect-ratio, simply because such a wing has relatively more tip area. Such losses are much more serious for fast-flying bats because with their small wings and high wing loadings, they cannot 'afford' to lose much lift. Hence it is the fast-flying bats which have high aspect-ratio wings, particularly the molossids such as *Eumops*, but also some of the faster vespertilionids like *Lasiurus*. These bats hunt either in open areas or above the tree tops, and it is again interesting to note that the birds of similar habits, swifts and martins, also have high aspect-ratio wings. For slow-flying bats, extreme aerodynamic efficiency is less important than manoeuvrability in confined spaces, and these bats usually have more compact wings of low aspect-ratio.

One other important variable is the size of the tail and uropatagium. Insectivorous and predatory bats generally have quite a large tail and a well developed uropatagium; many fruit-eating bats, both pteropodids and phyllostomids, have no tail and practically no uropatagium. The reason for the difference is not entirely clear, but insectivorous bats do use the uropatagium in flight as a pouch to hold insects; fruit bats can handle their food with their thumbs. This is only part of the story, for bats of similar feeding habits may differ considerably in tail size. The large, carnivorous *Vampyrum spectrum* (Phyllostomidae) is tailless, yet the closely related *Chrotopterus auritus*, also believed to be a carnivore, has a large tail; the carnivorous Megadermatidae have a large uropatagium, though no visible tail. It is likely that the uropatagium plays an important aerodynamic function, perhaps assisting rapid manoeuvring in the same way as the movable parts of an aircraft's tail surfaces; this would be especially important for insectivorous bats.

What speeds can bats attain, and what is their load-carrying capacity? Many species can fly at very low speeds and even hover, but the data on fast flying are limited. Hayward and Davis (1964) and Patterson and Hardin (1969) managed to obtain some speeds for bats flying along artificial tunnels, and they also quote figures from other sources. Between them, they found that eight species of *Myotis* could fly at speeds between 8 and 13 metres per second (around 20–30mph). *Pipistrellus hesperus* was somewhat slower (5 metres per second). The fastest under these conditions was the big brown bat *Eptesicus fuscus*, which flew at 15 metres per second. This speed compares well with a speed of 14 metres per second (31mph) reported for the noctule (*Nyctalus noctula*) as recorded by a car speedometer, and for *Miniopterus schreibersi* as judged from homing experiments. Three species of *Tadarida*, which one would

43

expect to be fast flying, were disappointing, flying at only 8–10 metres per second, but then bats which are adapted and accustomed to flying in open areas might not fly at full speed enclosed in a somewhat unfamiliar tunnel. Measurements in the open would be better in this respect, and indeed Patterson and Hardin report that *Eptesicus fuscus* flying in the open clocked 21 metres per second (40mph), the fastest speed reported for any bat.

The trouble with speed measurements taken in the open (including this one) is that the bat may be diving or flying with a tail wind, either of which would help it to reach much higher speeds than it could attain by itself in level flight. Bird flight speeds are also poorly known.

The weight-carrying abilities of bats are a bit better known, due to the obliging nature of a few individuals of different species. The champion might be expected among species with a low wing-loading, but is probably the female red bat *Lasiurus borealis* found by Stains (1965). She weighed 12.9g, and probably had a wing loading of about 0.09g per square centimetre; she was carrying four young, whose weight totalled 23.4g. Not surprisingly she was unable to take off, but she presumably flew to where she was found and carried there a load totalling 181 per cent of her own weight! Bats of other species have been recorded with loads, of young, of embryos, or (in autumn) of fat reserves equal to between 25 and 50 per cent of their (summer) body weight.

Davis and Cockrum (1964) conducted an interesting series of experiments in which they loaded bats with lead shot until they were just unable to take off. As with the attempts to measure flight speed, this probably resulted in unrealistic measurements for some species. *Tadarida brasiliensis*, for example, only lifted 9.3 per cent of its body weight, but this bat normally launches itself into flight by diving from a cave roof or crevice. This method does probably give useful results for species which regularly land to pick up prey. The champion in their experiments was a female long-eared bat (*Plecotus townsendii*) of 10.1g, which managed to lift 7.4g or 73.3 per cent of her own weight.

CHAPTER 3

FOOD AND FEEDING

The ancestral Chiroptera were insectivorous, judging by their teeth and evolutionary background, but modern bats have developed a wide range of feeding habits. The fundamental similarity in structure of all bats has meant that for the group to expand into new habitats, with more than just one or two species, there has been a greater evolutionary incentive to develop different feeding habits than in most other mammalian orders. Bats have established themselves in most of the major mammalian feeding niches accessible to them, and developed one (drinking blood) which is unique among terrestrial vertebrates (Table 3).

No bat has become truly herbivorous in the way the rodents have, perhaps because the digestion of grass and leaves depends upon the breakdown of cellulose by micro-organisms (like composting or fermentation), and the voluminous alimentary tract this requires, so prominent in rodents and ungulates, would result in a bulky rotund abdomen inappropriate for a flying mammal (there are plenty of herbivorous birds, but most of them are fairly large).

Tropical regions support a broader spectrum of feeding habits, but in all regions aerial insect-feeding is the most common (Wilson, 1973).

Food and Feeding

In each of the main zoogeographical regions, bats have evolved specialisations to exploit the different types of food available.

TABLE 3

Analysis of bat species by diet. The figures are approximate, because the diet of many species is known only by inference from their tooth structure and the habits of their better-known relatives; also some species eat more than one type of food. (Based upon Koopman & Knox Jones, 1970.)

Diet	Approx % of total bat species	Families represented
Insects	70	Most
Fruit	23	Pteropodidae & Phyllostomidae
Nectar and pollen	5·3	Pteropodidae & Phyllostomidae
Blood	0·3	Desmodontidae
Fish/aquatic insects	0·6	Noctilionidae & Vespertilionidae
Small vertebrates	0·7	Megadermatidae & Phyllostomidae

This has led to some fine examples of convergent evolution, where unrelated animals have come to resemble each other having developed similar adaptations for the same way of life. For example, flat crowned teeth and a ridged palate have been independently acquired by the fruit-eating bats of the Old World (Pteropodidae) and the New (Phyllostomidae). The habit of foliage gleaning, picking insects off trees and bushes, is found in a variety of bats in the Palaearctic, Nearctic and Neotropical regions; but the different species involved all have large ears, broad wings and slow manoeuvrable flight. (Interestingly this feeding method, a major one in birds, is little developed in bats as a whole.) In the spear-nosed bats (Phyllostomidae) a wide spectrum of feeding habits and adaptations has evolved within the single family (fig 11).

The bats of temperate regions remain almost exclusively insectivorous, but in the tropics there is a greater diversity, more marked in the New World than in the Old. The general tendency

46

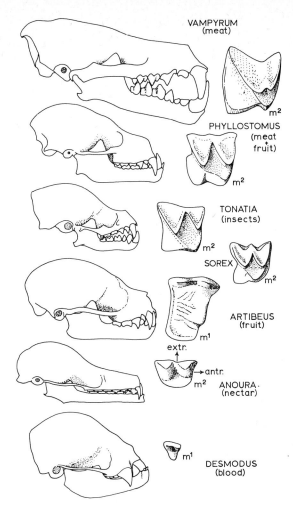

Fig 11. Skulls of various members of the Phyllostomidae and the closely related *Desmodus*, showing adaptations to different diets. Also shown is a single upper right molar, in surface view. The insectivorous *Tonatia* is probably the basic type and its cheek teeth very similar to those of shrews (*Sorex*). The omnivorous *Phyllostomus* is remarkably similar, but the truly carnivorous *Vampyrum* has a massive face and large canines. The frugivorous *Artibeus* has a short face, but its cheek teeth are very broad to provide more fruit-crushing surface. *Anoura* has an elongate face and poorly developed teeth. A blood diet requires no chewing and the tiny molars of *Desmodus* are very simple in form.

47

for tropical ecosystems to promote a proliferation of separate species, all living in the same place, is certainly evident in tropical forests and their bat faunas. In Trinidad, for instance, three species of *Artibeus* occur: *A. jamaicensis*, *A. lituratus* and *A. cinereus*. All feed on fruit, seemingly in close competition with each other *and* in the presence of at least eleven other species of frugivorous bats. However, the three *Artibeus* differ greatly in size (averaging about 40, 65 and 12g respectively), and may thus avoid mutual competition by exploiting different sizes of food items.

Bats gain further ecological separation by exploiting different strata in the forest canopy and by foraging over open ground or over still water. McNab (1971) analysed bat faunas on isolated Caribbean islands and concluded that the food resources were shared according to type and particle size among a basic 'set' of bat types, consisting of one fruit-eating species, two nectar feeders, two insect feeders and one fishcatcher; and each island's fauna included so many of these 'sets'.

Among insectivorous bats, whose prey is small and caught at high speed, the potential for selective feeding and avoidance of competition is less. Although there is some differentiation, based upon size of insects, the sizes taken by one bat species will overlap with those caught by others. Summer densities of insects may allow plenty for all, competition perhaps becoming serious only in the colder months. At such times bats hibernate or migrate; some species may even take other types of food. Competition with insectivorous birds is not usually significant, since the birds feed during the daytime and the bats mainly at night. It is interesting that Poulton (1929), in his survey of prey taken by British bats, identified 1,228 moths of which all but 16 were cryptically coloured. Evidently these species avoided predation by birds during the day, but did not escape capture by bats at night, when their camouflage was no help to them.

Food and Feeding

INSECTIVOROUS BATS

The majority of bats have retained the primitive habit of feeding on insects. This naturally imposes certain limitations, especially upon the species of higher latitudes, since insects are not uniformly abundant throughout the year. Even in the tropics, dry seasons are often accompanied by a marked dearth of insects. Yet insectivorous bats manage quite successfully, and in favourable regions may become exceptionally numerous; the famous American guano bat (*Tadarida brasiliensis*) was estimated to number 100 million in Texas alone (Davis *et al.* 1962) in 1957, though it is much less abundant now. The ecological impact of such numbers of insect predators must be considerable though it has been little investigated, partly because of the difficulty of identifying precisely what insects a bat has eaten. Logic suggests that large bats will probably eat bigger insects than small bats. It is also likely that since bats fly at night nocturnal species will predominate in their diet, rather than abundant but diurnal insects such as butterflies, damselflies and wasps.

Fortunately, the 'outer casing' of insects consists of chitin, one of nature's most indestructible products. Chemically it is an amino-polysaccharide, which resists digestive destruction, leaving identifiable fragments in the gut and faeces of predators. (The gastric juices of horseshoe bats have been shown to contain a chitinase; but digested chitin probably adds little to the nutrient value of the diet, though the partial destruction of chitin may well help to break down chewed food and speed digestion as a whole.) To identify precisely what a bat has eaten requires painstaking and skilled microscopical examination of the thousands of chewed-up fragments found in its stomach or faeces. Most researchers prefer more alluring tasks, especially as bats chew their food finer than almost any other insectivorous animal. Some of the studies of bat diets were reviewed by Allen (1939), who cited for example Hamilton's (1933) work on the American big brown bat (*Eptesicus fuscus*), or rather on 2,200 of its faecal pellets. These were soaked, teased apart and the tiny bits of insect legs, wings and mouthparts were identified as fully as possible. Among the number of identifiable insect fragments a variety of orders were represented in the following proportions:

	Recognisable fragments—%
Beetles (Coleoptera)	36·1—mostly scarabs
Social insects (Hymenoptera)	26·3—includes flying ants
Flies (Diptera)	13·2—mostly houseflies
Stoneflies (Plecoptera)	6·5
Mayflies (Ephemeroptera)	4·6
Bugs (Hemiptera)	3·4
Caddis flies (Trichoptera)	3·2
Lacewings (Neuroptera)	3·2
Scorpion flies (Mecoptera)	2·7
Crickets & cockroaches (Orthoptera)	0·6

It would be tempting to regard this, and similar analyses, as a statement of the proportional composition of a bat's diet, but it is not, for two good reasons. Firstly the list only shows the proportional representation of the *insects that were identified*. Some insects have very solid structures, such as jaws, head capsules and leg segments, that remain recognisable even after being chewed up and swallowed; but many groups of soft-bodied insects may be almost completely consumed, leaving little or no detectable remnants in the bat faeces. It is notable that beetles (whose forewings, elytra, form such characteristic shiny fragments in bat droppings) predominate among the groups recognised, and the decreasing proportion of the other groups closely parallels their decreasing hardness and durability.

Secondly, such an analysis fails to allow for the differences in size and nutritional content of the various prey items. For instance, if a bat eats 100 midges but gets twice as much nutritional benefit from a couple of juicy moths, a purely numerical analysis wrongly suggests that midges were 50 times more important. Some insects contain large deposits of stored fat, others characteristically have a large exoskeleton and little meat inside. Simple food catalogues of this type also obscure seasonal (or even

Page 51 (left) The largest American bat, Vampyrum spectrum, is carnivorous, feeding on mice, gekkos and small bats; (below) the ridged palate and smooth crowned molars of an Old World fruit bat (Rousettus)

Page 52 (right) The frugivorous phyllostomid bat *Uroderma* from tropical South America has unusually bold markings on its fur; (*below*) the long-eared freetailed bat, *Otomops martiensseni*, from East Africa. Its ferocious appearance is only a threat display

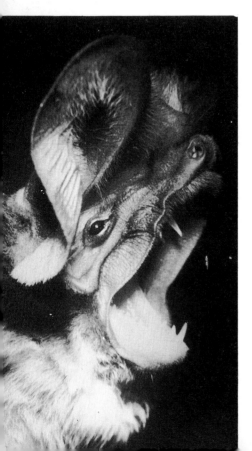

daily) variations in diet, unless regular samples are taken from the same place over an extended period.

Broad comparisons show that some bats eat a lot of moths, whereas others specialise more in beetle-catching. Many species are opportunist, taking whatever insects are most abundant at the time. An extensive study of the feeding ecology of eighteen species of insectivorous bats by Ross (1967), in the south-western USA, revealed that moths, beetles and grasshoppers constituted the bulk of the food taken. Relatively few Diptera (flies) were encountered in his analyses, though they are often presumed to be a major food item of bats. One of the largest North American bats, *Macrotus californicus*, was revealed as a predator of big moths and crickets, and apparently picked food off the leaves of trees. The pallid bat (*Antrozous pallidus*) fed on large things, mostly over 17mm long; and scorpions and flightless ground-living insects figured in its diet, suggesting that it had alighted to capture its prey. Direct observations revealed that this species flies low (15–100cm) over the ground. It pounces on its prey, then flies away with it: a difficult feat, but less surprising than its ability to avoid fatal retaliation from the scorpions!

Ross found a considerable range in the size of insects taken by any one species, which may reflect different hunting methods. Large moths and beetles are almost certainly pursued individually using echolocation (see Chapter 7), perhaps aided by sight. If bats always detect their prey by echolocation, then the nature of the bat's ultrasonics will govern the effective resolution of different-sized prey items and affect the size of prey taken. Bats seem not to catch insects smaller than the wavelength of the ultrasounds used to locate them (Gould, 1955), but there is some argument whether small insects are caught by the mouthful, the bat dashing into dense swarms with its mouth open, performing almost as a filter feeder in 'aerial plankton'. Experiments with captive little brown bats (*Myotis lucifugus*) revealed that some could catch tiny fruit flies, and in a given time-interval the number accumulated in a bat's stomach was similar to the number of 'terminal-phase' ultrasonic buzzes (associated with final stage of prey pursuit) picked up by a bat detector. This is taken to suggest that even these abnormally small food items are located and pursued singly.

However, observations on captive *M. lucifugus* may not apply to dissimilar species living under natural conditions. Ross found one western pipistrelle (*Pipistrellus hesperus*) which still had four black-flies in its mouth when shot, indicating at least one multiple capture; furthermore, tooth marks and damage to insects recovered from stomachs showed that prey had been taken from all angles. In contrast, moths eaten by other bats all showed signs of similar treatment: approach from the rear, abdomen bitten off, wings and head discarded just as one would expect if the prey had been individually tracked and caught.

The sheer numbers of small insects taken in only half an hour suggest that they are not pursued individually, and if insects are present in sufficient densities why should the bat not take two or three (or even more) at once? One snag would be that a mouthful of insects would hamper echolocation, but larger species that habitually carry big moths or crickets back to a feeding roost seem to manage successfully.

Echolocation would provide extra assistance for locating dense swarms or pursuing individual big prey items. Nyholm (1965) was able to catch bats in a trap baited with a bag full of buzzing bluebottles! One further point, often overlooked, is that the insects themselves are not silent. We can easily hear and locate the buzz of a bee or fly; perhaps the extra sensitivity of a bat's ears enables it to hear the faint whine of a midge or rustle of a tiny moth?

Flight patterns may affect diet. Among British bats, noctules (*Nyctalus noctula*) fly fast and high, making occasional swoops to snatch some desirable prey item. Pipistrelles (*P. pipistrellus*) flutter rapidly with dizzy gyrations two or three metres above the ground; and Daubenton's bat (*Myotis daubentoni*) sometimes flies straight and very low above the surface of still water, searching for emerging aquatic insects. The long-eared bat (*Plecotus*) hovers among the branches of trees, picking insects from the foliage. Such behaviour would enable it to eat caterpillars and arachnids, unlikely to be taken by fast-flying bats.

The American genera *Macrotus* and *Antrozous* are also big-eared and have low-intensity sonar (like *Plecotus*). Their feeding method is similar and they habitually alight to feed on the ground (*Antrozous* has even been caught in a mousetrap!). The larger size of potential prey and the absence of competition for it may well compensate for the difficulties of landing and take-off (and locating insects among stones, leaves and other obstructions). Pouncing on one fat grasshopper might be easier than chasing an equivalent amount of food in the form of hundreds of flies, especially if the latter had to be shared with many other more conventional insectivorous bats. The African species *Nycteris thebaica* takes scorpions off the ground; it is also big-eared and similar in build to *Antrozous*.

Many bats which catch their insects in flight often use the wing to brush larger prey towards the mouth (fig 12). The food is some-

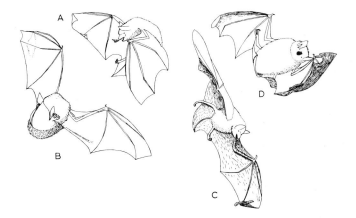

Fig 12. Insectivorous bats may catch insects conventionally in the mouth, A, but large insects may be transferred to the tail pouch, B for dismembering. Sometimes when prey seems likely to escape they will also use the wings to catch it, C, D. (Based on Webster & Griffin, 1962.)

times transferred to the tail, which is pulled forwards to form a pouch. The insect is held there and eaten, the bat bending its head down to the tail whilst still in flight. When the insects, such as crickets and moths, are too large or unwieldy for this treatment they are carried back to a favourite perch and dismembered, the soft body being eaten and the wings and legs discarded. An impressive pile of insect litter may accumulate below the feeding roost as evidence of the bat's picnic. At one house we visited a bat used to hang from a nail in the wall while it dismembered a variety of moths in the shelter of the porch. After a few nights, 49 moth wings were collected, representing remains from 12 fat-bodied noctuid species.

In captivity, bats react to distasteful insects by spitting them out in obvious disgust. In the wild they must do this quite often, for at night they could not recognise the warning colouring that usually deters would-be predators. Perhaps distasteful insects produce distinctive sounds or echoes that enable bats to steer clear of them? Some moths (Arctiidae) emit clicking noises which inhibit the bat's pursuit of them; they are also unpleasantly flavoured. Others, not necessarily distasteful, can hear the bat's ultrasonic emissions and react by taking avoiding action: some fold their wings and drop like a stone, others go spiralling fast and erratically towards the ground just like a World War II fighter pilot spinning away to get the enemy off his tail.

Considering that the bat hunts insects at high speed, in the dark, probably using sound patterns to locate them, its success is remarkable. Gould (1955) found that *Myotis lucifugus* could catch over 1g of insects in an hour (representing perhaps 500 individual captures) and *Pipistrellus subflavus* could catch a quarter of its own weight of insects in thirty minutes. The huge population of *Tadarida brasiliensis* in Texas may account for over 6,600 tons of insects per year!

Finding approximately how much food is eaten during the night is not too difficult. By comparing the weight of insects fed to a captive bat with the weight of faeces produced as a result, a 'food conversion ratio' may be calculated. Multiplying this by the weight of faeces collected (say on a clean polythene sheet) from below a bat roost after a known time-interval, will provide a rough guide to the quantity of food represented by the droppings. Naturally, collection of faeces at a roost makes no allowance for any voided elsewhere.

Insects are a fairly nutritious kind of food, but just how much effort an insectivorous bat spends in getting them, how long and how far it flies in a night, are unknown, mainly because of the difficulties of making such studies in the dark.

New techniques such as the use of bat detectors and miniature radio transmitters (discussed in Chapters 6 & 7) may help at least to show where the bats go to feed. In a recent investigation of pond bats, infra-red binoculars were used and the bats marked with reflective sticky tape to make them more conspicuous (Voute, 1972). The bats left their roost in a church and followed distinct, regularly used routes to their hunting areas, which extended for 6 miles along a few canals. Here they would feed, spending much time hunting around conspicuous objects such as bridges and overhanging trees. Two other insectivorous species (*Myotis daubentoni* and *M. mystacinus*) were studied in Finland; in this 'land of the midnight sun' summer 'nights' are still light enough to permit direct observation of bat hunting behaviour (Nyholm, 1965). Feeding areas for these species were usually close (maximum 700 metres) to the roost, but changed seasonally. In early summer, *M. mystacinus* frequented woodland, each bat hunting over an exclusive territory of about 240 square metres. Later in summer, insects were pursued in more open areas, each bat enlarging its range to over 5,000 square metres, but overlapping with others. Hunting territories remained remarkably constant from year to year.

In contrast to these local patrols by small *Myotis* species, the fast-flying American guano bats are thought to journey up to 50 miles on a night's feeding excursion (Davis *et al.* 1962). They would need to consume a considerable quantity of insects just to recoup the energy spent in travelling.

CARNIVOROUS BATS

Although insectivorous bats might be regarded as carnivorous in the broad sense, some bats prey upon quite large vertebrates, including other bats. Certain insectivorous rhinolophids and vespertilionids may occasionally feel moved to catch bigger prey, but two groups of large bats regularly do so. The Old World family Megadermatidae ('false vampires') are large, long-eared, frequently savage beasts. *Megaderma* species live in Africa and Asia; *Macroderma* (largest of the Microchiroptera) inhabits the tropical parts of Australia. Several of the megadermatids catch small rodents, bats, frogs and birds (mainly small species such as white-eyes and sunbirds), and some will even enter houses to pluck gekkos from the walls. The megadermatids can land on the ground and take off again without difficulty, and often carry their prey to a favourite perch or roost, where they leave a macabre litter of tiny skulls and bones.

The New World carnivorous bats belong to the dominant South American family, the Phyllostomidae. For example, *Phyllostomus hastatus* is a large species which feeds on fruit but also regularly takes mammals and birds. A captive one ate 25 mice, 13 bats, 3 birds and some bananas in $5\frac{1}{2}$ months. But the real hunter is *Vampyrum spectrum*. With a 90cm (3ft) wing-span, this is the largest American bat. It is almost entirely carnivorous. Stomach analyses have revealed fur of rodents and bats, plus the feathers and bones of many birds, including doves. In captivity it eagerly devours meat, mice and even small chickens. A pair fed four mice each per night were observed to clutch the dead rodents with the thumb claw and carry them to the top of the cage (Goodwin & Greenhall, 1961), where the head was eaten first and the tail discarded. We have seen captive *Vampyrum* in Trinidad consume *Phyllostomus hastatus* (itself a large bat) in great quantity with gory relish, leaving behind only the jaws, feet and a few shreds of wings and tail.

PISCIVOROUS BATS

At least two species of bats, *Noctilio leporinus* and *Pizonyx vivesi*, feed principally on fish. The latter frequents the coastal regions of Baja California and Mexico, the former species occurs over much of Central America and extends south to Argentina. The fisherman bat, *Noctilio*, is the better-known. It is upwards of 10cm long, with short sparse fur and long legs. The enormous feet bear very long hooked claws which are used to scoop fish from the water as the bat flies low over the surface. It hunts over fresh water and calm sea, taking fish, often anchovies, which are small and usually shoal at the surface in large numbers. The bat may eat its catch in flight, making clearly audible crunching noises, or carry the fish in its mouth to a convenient perch. In captivity, *Noctilio* has been known to eat 30 to 40 small fish per night, but in the wild would probably average rather fewer, as windy nights or heavy rain must seriously affect its catch.

There was some controversy about how *Noctilio* manages to detect the presence of fish. It has now been shown that it uses echolocation to detect not the fish themselves, but the ripples they cause at the surface (see Chapter 7). The bat will scoop its feet into any likely disturbance in the water which it can easily detect from patterns of reflected sound.

The bats must get wet during their fishing activities and occasionally they fall into the water, but they can swim well and their short greasy fur does not become waterlogged. They do run the risk of the tables being turned—there are reports of fishing bats being eaten by carnivorous fish!

Pizonyx vivesi is less well known and in captivity has not cooperated so readily with investigators seeking to discover how it manages to feed. In the wild it is often gregarious, like *Noctilio*, inhabiting caves and crevices, but it also lives under stones and seashore debris. Like *Noctilio* it has enormous feet, with very narrow hooked claws and is presumed to use them in a similar way.

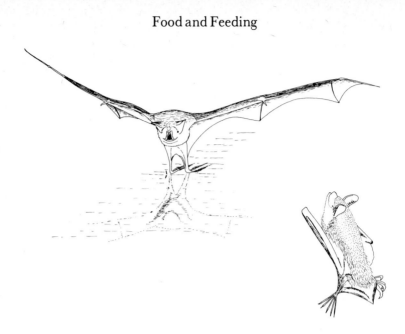

Fig 13. Two fish-eating bats: *Noctilio* (left) trailing its claws in the water; *Pizonyx* (right) shows the very large hind feet characteristic of piscivorous bats (from photographs in Suthers, 1965 and Walker, 1968)

Megaderma lyra of Asia has also been reported to take fish among its more usual vertebrate prey, but megadermatids are not modified for fishing and perhaps should not be regarded as truly piscivorous. Various other bats regularly forage low over water. The European Daubenton's bat (*Myotis daubentoni*), for example, flies within an inch or so of the surface, taking aquatic invertebrates (eg Ostracods) and emergent insects, and has recently been reported to catch small fish as well (Brosset & Debouttenville, 1966). Perhaps bats with similar habits occasionally pick up the odd fish, or maybe in catching aquatic invertebrates at the surface they represent a stage in the evolution of the fishing habit which was passed through by the ancestors of *Noctilio* and *Pizonyx* in their efforts to exploit a new food source and escape competition from more conventional bats.

SANGUIVOROUS BATS

Written records of 'blood-sucking' bats have existed since Columbus landed in Trinidad in 1498, and in the sixteenth century, during their conquest of Central America, the Spaniards reported that they were much troubled by bats which sought the blood of men and horses at night.

These relatively modest accounts have become intermixed with a proliferation of horrific tales, including those concerning Count Dracula and his friends the 'vampires' in quasi-human form: timorous maidens would sleep uneasily at night lest a few of them elected to pop across from Transylvania on a sanguivorous sortie. Not only did bats in general acquire a thoroughly distasteful reputation, but the name 'vampire' was assigned to a range of dissimilar and inappropriate species, causing a confusion that still remains.

The true vampires constitute the family Desmodontidae. They feed exclusively on the blood of warm-blooded animals, and are the only vertebrates to do so; this is probably the most extreme dietary specialisation among the Chiroptera. There are just three species, confined to Central and South America, with *Desmodus rotundus* the most widespread.

Vampires are extraordinarily agile on the ground, raising themselves up high on their wrists and feet, hopping and scurrying about like huge spiders. Using this unique ability, they approach a sleeping victim, having alighted some distance away. *Desmodus* usually attacks cattle, probably because they are easy to locate, docile and often tethered. *Diphylla* and *Diaemus* are more attracted to chickens.

Their liquid diet requires no mastication, so vampires have fewer teeth than other bats (twenty in *Desmodus*). The molars are simple and pointed, lacking any flat grinding surface. Only the needle-sharp blade-like incisors and upper canines are actually used (fig 14), making a swift, scooping bite, usually in an area where the skin is thin and has many blood vessels close to the surface. Such places (ears, neck, anal region) tend to be warmer because of their enhanced blood flow and may actually attract the bat. Vampires do not suck blood: they lap it up as it flows freely from the wound; meanwhile saliva trickles down the underside of the bat's tongue and into the wound. Recent work (Hawkey, 1966) has demonstrated that the saliva contains an anticoagulant substance which retards clotting and promotes the continued flow of blood. The vampire is thus assured of a plentiful supply, and the victim is usually unaware of its involuntary largesse until it wakes up.

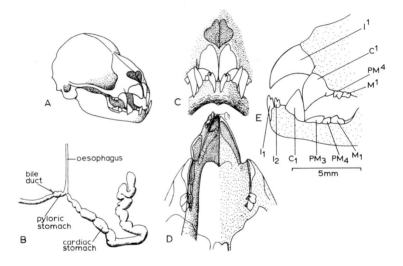

Fig 14. Adaptations of the vampire *Desmodus rotundus*. The skull, A, shows enlarged upper incisors which gouge out a divot of flesh and the sharp canines probably used to shave the fur from a suitable spot. The stomach, B, has a remarkably elongated cardiac region which stores the blood meal. C, D, E show details of dentition (the lower dentition superimposed on the left side of D). The bilobed lower incisors function as a fur comb. The cheek teeth are almost useless.

Vampires will often return several nights in succession to the same victim and up to fourteen bats have been observed feeding simultaneously from the same horse.

Captive *Desmodus* studied by Wimsatt & Guerriere (1962) drank so much blood they could scarcely fly. Such engorgement is essential if the bat is to get sufficient solids in its liquid diet to provide adequate nourishment. The bats begin to urinate very soon, often whilst still drinking, as their short simple intestine sets about reducing the fluid content of their meal. Captives drink about 15ml of blood per night, often imbibing their full quota in a matter of twenty minutes or so. In the wild they feed only in the early part of the night, the average foraging time away from the roost being about two hours, and may consume 30ml or more, up to one and a half times their own weight (Wimsatt, 1969b). It is estimated that a single bat drinks at least 7 litres per year. At this rate, a colony of 100 bats would each year lap up the entire blood volume of 25 cows or over 14,000 chickens! These estimates are based upon the consumption of captive vampires who are relatively inactive and might take less than they would in the wild. Furthermore, no allowance is made for the prolonged bleeding of vampire bites, due to the application of anticoagulant saliva, which may double the volume of blood actually lost as a result of the bat's activity.

FRUGIVOROUS BATS

Fruit-eating bats are inhabitants of the tropics, especially the forest regions, for it is here that, in the consistently high humidity and high temperatures, at least some species of trees are in fruit in every month of the year.

The frugivorous habit has been developed independently in two quite separate lines: in the true fruit bats of the Old World (Megachiroptera: Pteropodidae) and, in their absence from the New World, certain members of the microchiropteran family Phyllostomidae. In complete geographical and evolutionary isolation from one another, these two groups have developed almost identical specialisations for their common way of life.

The bats seek out soft, ripe fruits by smell, even raiding fruit bowls in people's houses! Their predilection for mangoes, figs, guavas, bananas and other commercially valuable types may result in their being regarded as pests, but they mainly eat wild fruits and berries in the forests. Sometimes the bats hover whilst taking bites, they may hang from a convenient nearby branch, and some species carry fruit away.

Fruits are crushed in the mouth, only the juices and soft pulp being swallowed; in some species the oesophagus is only 2 or 3mm wide, so only liquid food *could* be swallowed. The seeds, skins and fibrous material are compressed into a pellet and spat out, aided by morphological modifications of the mouth: the teeth are smooth, broad and aided in their simple crushing function by the muscular tongue which forces the fruit against a series of sharp transverse ridges on the palate. These adaptations are seen in both the true fruit bats and the frugivorous phyllostomids (especially *Artibeus*). In both groups the food passes right through the short, simple digestive tract in a mere twenty minutes or so. There can thus be little or no bacterial breakdown of the food, so vital to most herbivorous mammals but unnecessary for bats whose food consists almost entirely of water and various natural sugars, the most readily digestible of all substances. The relative lack of chemical digestion results in the faeces retaining the characteristically fruity smell of the original food,—and provides a fruit-bat roost with very distinctive air.

The bat happily munching bananas has diverged far from the insectivorous feeding habits of its ancestors, though it is easy to see how frugivorous habits could have evolved. Ripe fruits tend to attract insects and may already have insect larvae burrowing in them. Perhaps certain bats took to feeding on the congregations of insects and inevitably ingested quantities of the sweet, juicy fruit. The fruit pulp, being highly nutritious and rather tasty, may then gradually have become an increasingly major part of the bat's diet. (An insectivorous African bat (*Hipposideros commersoni*) has been reported to attack figs which were later found to contain weevil larvae.)

The most extreme modifications are in those species which feed on the nectar and pollen of certain flowers: seven megachiropteran genera (sub-family Macroglossinae, eg *Eonycteris*) and various small phyllostomids of the sub-family Glossophaginae (especially *Anoura*, *Glossophaga* and *Choeronycteris*). These can be maintained in captivity solely on a liquid diet, though in the wild they may consume tiny insects and small amounts of fruit pulp. They are characterised by having a long protrusible tongue which may be one-third the length of the head and body, and often bears tufts of hairs or barbs near its tip, so that when it is pushed deep into flowers it picks up quantities of pollen as well as nectar. The stomachs of some bats have been found crammed full of pollen grains, derived especially from deep trumpet-shaped flowers. The teeth are minute, as would be expected with a diet of this sort, and when fed fruit pulp the bats make little or no attempt to chew it.

Once again there is an extraordinary similarity between the two groups in the Old World and the New. In a sense, both groups parallel the sunbirds and humming birds in their respective hemispheres; they live in areas where blossoms can be found all the time, and they hover before the flowers using their long tongues to lap up syrupy nectar, the most energy-rich of all foods. Birds exploit the flowers by day and bats work the night shift.

BAT FEEDING BIOLOGY AND THE ECOSYSTEM

By virtue of their feeding habits, bats often play a key role in the ecology of certain major habitats, aiding in the dispersal or suppression of various species and promoting the energy flow of certain ecosystems.

The most straightforward type of interaction is between insectivorous bats and their prey. As in other predator-prey relationships, the bats may effect a certain measure of control over the populations on which they feed. Some of the really big bat colonies must tend to deplete the food supply within normal foraging range, especially when thousands of newly weaned juveniles emerge. As the bats congregate in the Carlsbad caverns of New

Mexico prior to migration, guano production begins to decline whilst numbers of bats are still increasing, suggesting that food resources are beginning to run out.

Many of the frugivorous bats, despite their depredations, may actually promote the development and dispersal of the species on which they feed. Pips and seeds are spat out undamaged, often some distance from where the fruit was actually collected and thick forests of seedlings may develop in the rich dung below the bat feeding-roosts. Plant dispersal by bats (chiropterochory) may be of prime importance in tropical forests.

The whole subject of pollination and seed dispersal by bats has been reviewed by Van der Pijl (1957), who suggested that the evolution of fruit-bearing trees has proceeded in harmony with that of the bats that feed upon them. Dispersal of plants by bats is not just something that might happen occasionally by chance; it *must* happen, often. Many fruits could not be dispersed any other way. Many tropical trees and shrubs have become adapted for chiropterochory: their fruits have a strong fetid odour attractive to frugivorous bats and remain on the tree long after they are ripe, rather than fall to the ground for dispersal by terrestrial agents. 'Bat fruits' are often on long stalks positioned away from twigs and leaves, so that they are only accessible to hovering bats, not to perching birds. The fruits themselves are frequently furnished with a large hard kernel, which cannot be swallowed but readily separates from the fleshy pericarp and so is easily dropped to the ground. Other fruits (eg figs) have very tiny seeds which are resistant to digestion. These may be swallowed and carried internally before being voided to germinate elsewhere.

Flowering and fruiting seasons of individual tree species are staggered so that different fruits are available at different times of year, rather than being produced all at once in a glut. The bats are thus able to feed from each species in turn, disperse its seeds and move on to the next type of fruit as it comes into season: both the bats and the plants benefit. There is room in the system for frugivorous birds too, since they take mainly the conspicuous bright-coloured fruits and berries.

There is one further twist to the story. The plant would derive no benefit from having its seeds carried away to a bat's roost in a cave too dark for plant growth. But the true fruit bats (Megachiroptera), with only one exception, lack the ability to echolocate, so they cannot negotiate subterranean darkness and hence do not live in caves. The frugivorous Microchiroptera can echolocate, but few live in caves; most hang in trees.

Some of the nectivorous bats also have an important role in the cross-pollination of their food plants. Twenty or more genera, mostly trees and shrubs, depend wholly or mainly upon bats for the pollination of their flowers (the American calabash tree, *Crescentia*, the silk cotton trees, *Ceiba* and *Bombax*, various night-blooming cacti, wild bananas and the African baobab tree for instance). Just as the bats are modified for their flower-feeding habits by having a long muzzle and long protrusible tongue with a brushlike tip, so the flowers of these plants are usually strongly built, wide and deeply conical, unsuitable for pollination by insects but just right for a bat to insert its head and shoulders. They open only at night, when the bats are active but nectar-seeking birds are not. Most of these 'bat flowers' have a peculiar sickly smell and a copious supply of nectar.

Although bats may form an important link in the complex inter-relationships of a tropical forest, their importance in the subterranean world of caves is even more fundamental, since their feeding activities are often the basis of the whole food-web of the cave ecosystem. In caves, mines and similar underground habitats there is no natural light. Photosynthesis (the manufacture of starches and sugars by green plants in the presence of light) cannot take place, and all the food necessary to maintain the resident cave animals must be imported from elsewhere: a task performed by bats, whose droppings, deposited underground, form the total raw material supporting a complex flora and fauna. In cooler areas such as Britain, bats are usually too few to maintain large populations of cave animals, but in warmer regions with high bat densities vast quantities of dung can accumulate; up to 90 tons per year in certain Texan caves for instance.

The dung of insectivorous bats consists predominantly of indigestible insect chitin, which breaks down relatively slowly and is therefore not an ideal substrate for supporting armies of decomposers. Where there are some frugivorous bats adding their contribution of soft fruity dung, with plenty of carbohydrates, then the bat guano becomes a very rich source of food. Within the guano, an extensive fauna of decomposers, scavengers and their associated predators develops. They can easily live in the sheltered underground darkness, not needing light because they are entirely surrounded by food. Guano from frugivorous bats is mainly decomposed by fungi (moulds); insectivorous bat guano is primarily attacked by bacteria. The relative proportions of the two types therefore affect the relative numbers of fungal and bacterial feeders and their respective micro-predators. Sometimes decomposition of urine-soaked guano generates ammonia: in humans the maximum concentration of this endurable for only one hour is less than 100 parts per million, but some bats have adaptations in their respiratory system and blood chemistry which permit a high degree of ammonia tolerance. Guano bats tolerate ammonia concentrations of 5,000 parts per million, a level which kills mice in 10–20 minutes (Studier *et al.* 1967).

Caves with a bat-dung ecosystem can house very spectacular animal communities. In the vast Niah cave in Borneo for example, 1 million bats live with 4 million echolocating swiftlets (*Collocalia*), their dung and dead supporting an extraordinary range of life, including a unique wingless earwig (*Arixenia*) and a gecko found nowhere else in the world.

Another fine example of a tropical cave ecosystem based upon bat dung is in the Tamana cave of Central Trinidad, visited by one of us in 1969. The cave shelters tens of thousands of bats, belonging to eleven species; their food includes fruit, insects of various sizes, nectar, pollen and blood. A thick porridge of mixed droppings on the cave floor contains 20 per cent protein, is kept at a

Page 69 (above) A colony of serotines, *Eptesicus serotinus*, in a typical houseroof roost. The bats are hanging head-downwards from the roof ridge at the apex of the attic. Two of them are ringed; (*below*) young serotine bat before the growth of its fur. Note the large feet and head and the stubby wings

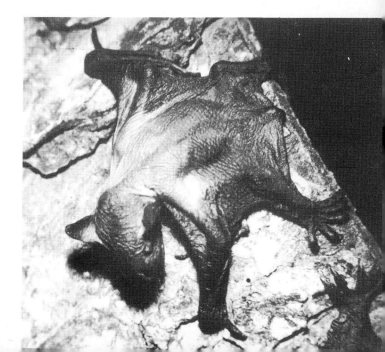

Page 70 (left) Tamana Cave, Trinidad, its air thick with eleven species of bat; *(right)* a bat box on the trunk of a tree. Note the entrance slit in the base, narrow to exclude birds

steaming 28°–30°C, and is permanently moistened by a small stream. A square metre may support over 1 million arthropods, including springtails, mites, millipedes, pseudoscorpions, insect larvae, beetles and isopods. The cockroaches alone (some over 5cm long) number several hundred to the square metre. The arthropods in turn provide food for large toads and the mountain crab, which lives in wall crevices consuming dead bats and other animals. The diptera larvae in the dung hatch into adult flies which are the food of *Phyllobates*, a small frog (whose tadpoles live in the stream feeding on bacteria from the dung), which is in turn preyed upon by the coral snake (*Leimadophis*). Occasionally opossums (*Didelphys virginianus*) enter the cave: although they presumably cannot see what they are doing in the darkness, they don't have to, being happy to eat any of the food that surrounds them on all sides. The whole Tamana cave is a seething, heaving mass of life in total darkness and a Turkish-bath atmosphere. Biologically it is fascinating, but from all other viewpoints utterly revolting!

CHAPTER 4

HIBERNATION

In the higher latitudes of both the northern and southern hemispheres, winter means a shortage of food, especially for insectivorous animals. In response to this, most insectivorous bats in these
regions hibernate, though some may migrate to warmer climates.
Hibernation is perhaps best seen as an important physiological
adaptation enabling them to survive in more extreme climatic
conditions than most other bats. Among small insectivorous
birds, the challenge of winter is usually met by migration rather
than hibernation (known bird hibernators so far include only two
species of nightjars).

These differing responses to the rigours of winter prompt a
number of questions: why don't more birds hibernate? Why don't
more bats migrate? If wrens, tree-creepers and titmice can remain
active all winter, why can't bats? But above all, just what is hibernation, what does it involve and how do bats manage to live at
body temperatures well below those which kill most other mammals, humans included?

WHAT IS HIBERNATION?

A bat found hibernating in a cave seems to be dead; its breathing is imperceptible, its heart-beat is so slow as to be easily over-looked, its body is cold to touch and often covered in droplets of condensed moisture. Physiological measurements would confirm these impressions; in a small bat, the oxygen consumption would be only 0.03 millilitres per gramme of body-weight per hour, com-pared with 3.0ml when active; the heart-rate, normally about 400 beats per minute (and over 1,000 beats per minute in flight), drops to about 25 beats per minute in hibernation; and the body temper-ature is only about 6°C, perhaps 1°C higher than that of the cool air in the cave, compared with 36°C when the bat is active, and about 41°C when it is flying. The respiratory quotient (see Chap-ter 2) of the hibernating bat would be about 0.7, indicating that fat is being metabolised; in other words, it would be living on the fat laid down during the autumn.

The remarkable thing about such an apparently moribund animal is that it is able to wake itself up; touching it, to feel its heart-beat or temperature, would almost certainly cause it to wake. Disturbance alone is often sufficient to cause arousal; the bat does not need external heat to restore it to the fully active state. It is in this respect that the physiology of a hibernating mammal differs from that of a hibernating cold-blooded animal like a frog; the bat can regain and maintain its normal body temperature, by its own heat production, whereas a frog is almost totally depen-dent on an outside source of heat to warm it up. The same feature distinguishes a hibernating bat from a mammal which is suffering hypothermia. If a normally warm-blooded mammal is exposed to prolonged cold and has insufficient food or fat reserves to produce enough compensatory heat, its body temperature drops, that is it enters hypothermia. This is usually what happens to climbers or explorers suffering from 'exposure'. Recovery is only possible if outside heat is applied, exactly as in a cold-blooded animal. Bats can and do suffer hypothermia (even species which normally hi-bernate) under experimental conditions, which further empha-sises that hibernation is a rather special physiological mechanism. One could argue that the terms 'hibernation' and 'hibernator' should not be used for cold-blooded animals like frogs at all, but restricted to those warm-blooded animals, like bats, which are able to rouse themselves from torpor without externally applied heat.

A 'warm-blooded' animal is in much the same thermodynamic state as a hot cup of tea in a cold room; it loses heat to the air around it at a rate that depends very largely on how much cooler that air is. The other factor which affects the rate of heat loss is the thermal conductance of the intervening material; the cooling of the tea can be slowed by putting a saucer over it, or pouring it into a vacuum flask, and the animal could grow a thicker coat, lay down an insulating layer of fat under the skin, curl up in a nest or, in our own case, put on a coat. We colloquially refer to such measures as attempts to keep warm, but in fact they only reduce the rate of cooling. Actually keeping warm, producing heat, requires the expenditure of energy. This is chemical energy, acquired by eating food; and its expenditure is the result of metabolism of the food (or fat) by oxygen taken in during respiration. A gramme of fat, oxidised completely, yields 9,300 calories, enough energy to heat a litre of water (and flesh is 80 per cent water!) from 25°C up to blood heat at 34°C. A gramme of sugar would yield 4,100 calories, and a gramme of protein slightly more (Green, 1969).

The warm-blooded animals (birds and mammals) differ from the others in being able to metabolise their food reserves sufficiently rapidly to maintain their high body temperatures in this way. Hibernating animals have a metabolic rate fast enough to keep their bodies at a high and fairly constant temperature, but during hibernation they do not use that ability, and so their body temperature falls.

Other factors are also relevant here. If the ambient temperature and the body temperature are the same, the animal need do no metabolic 'work' to keep warm. This is also true for ambient temperatures down to about 5°C below body temperature, because necessary metabolic work (eg the heart beating) will supply some 'waste' heat. The minimal level of metabolism is referred to as the basal metabolic rate (or BMR). At ambient temperatures *above* body temperature, the animal must use energy to keep cool (by perspiring, panting, or, in the case of a bat, fanning its wings), while at temperatures more than 5°C *below* body temperature, it must expend energy in keeping warm. This expenditure of energy is usually measured in terms of the amount of oxygen consumed per unit of body weight per unit of time; it is easier to measure oxygen uptake than other parameters like heat production, food stores lost, or carbon dioxide produced, but all these can similarly be used as indicators of metabolic rate.

Since the heat lost from a warm-blooded animal mostly escapes through the body surface, the loss is more acute for small animals than large ones, small animals having a much larger surface area in relation to body size. Most bats are fairly small and they have compounded the problem by possessing wings made of skin. As a result bats have the highest surface area, in proportion to their body-weight, of any vertebrate animal; thus their potential for losing body-heat is greatly increased.

Hibernation is often thought of simply as an extended, rather deep, sleep, but is in fact a much more complex physiological event. Far from just 'dozing off', a hibernator undergoes complex changes in its blood composition, hormone balance and immunological tolerance, in addition to the obvious slowing of its general metabolism. A full consideration of these would require a complex and controversial physiological study, and we will confine ourselves to those aspects which relate directly to bats.

THE HIBERNATORS

Generally speaking, bats are a tropical group, and have no difficulty maintaining their body temperature; there is enough food to produce metabolic heat, and anyway the difference between body and ambient temperature is seldom great. As an example, fig 15 shows the responses of the large (150g) megadermatid *Macroderma gigas* to experimental exposure at various ambient temperatures.

It maintained its body temperature between 35°C and 39°C (varying somewhat with the individual) in air temperatures from 35°C right down to 0°C (Leitner and Nelson, 1967). Its metabolic rate was minimal at ambient temperatures of 30°C to 35°C (basal metabolic rate = 0.94ml of oxygen per gramme body weight, per hour), and increased steadily up to 2.5ml at 10°C. Equally, the metabolic rate increased when the ambient temperature was raised above 35°C, reaching 1.4ml of oxygen per gramme per hour at 38°C; even so the body temperature increased to 40.6°C. It is generally much more difficult for an animal to cool itself than to keep warm, and this temperature was in fact fatal to one of the test animals.

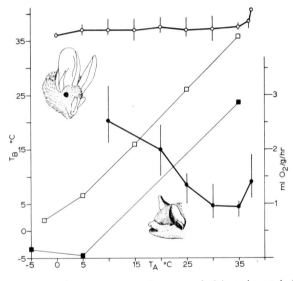

Fig 15. The body temperature (open symbols) and metabolic rate (closed symbols) for a homeothermic bat, *Macroderma gigas* (circles), and a hibernating bat, *Myotis sodalis* (squares), plotted against ambient temperature (T$_A$). (From Leitner and Nelson, 1967 and Henshaw, 1970.) When faced with lowered ambient temperatures, *Macroderma* raises its metabolic rate and produces enough heat to keep its body temperature at about 35°C. *Myotis* allows its metabolism and its body temperature to drop, only beginning to increase its metabolism slightly at temperatures near freezing point.

This experiment, and others like it, show that many bats are perfectly good homeotherms; well able to maintain a constant body temperature. Other megadermatids, pteropodids and most phyllostomids regulate their body temperature in the same way, although the smaller ones may be unable to maintain it in very cold conditions and are forced into hypothermia (often fatal).

For comparison, fig 15 shows the result of a similar experiment with *Myotis sodalis*, carried out in autumn, when the bat would be due to enter hibernation. When active and at an ambient temperature of 35°C, its metabolic rate was 1.71ml O_2/g/hr, but as the temperature of the experimental chamber was lowered the metabolic rate, instead of increasing, progressively declined, right down to 0.057ml at an ambient temperature of 5°C (when body temperature was about 6°C). However, when the air temperature was further lowered to −5°C, the animal's metabolic rate increased to 0.172ml O_2/g/hr (about the same as it was at 15°C), and its body temperature stayed just above 0°C; thus, this hibernator allowed its body to cool, following the ambient temperature down to freezing point but not below. This clearly emphasises the fact that a hibernating mammal is able to maintain its body temperature, but does not *have* to do so when conditions are less favourable, and will consume energy in order to prevent its temperature falling below freezing.

Other bats which enter hibernation in a similar way include representatives of the families Vespertilionidae, Rhinolophidae and perhaps also those molossids which inhabit temperate climates; together with at least some members of other families (probably Rhinopomatidae, Mystacinidae and Nycteridae, and *Macrotus* among the Phyllostomidae). Among non-chiropterans, the hedgehogs (Insectivora: Erinaceidae) and members of several rodent families, including the dormice (Muscardinidae), some ground squirrels and marmots (Sciuridae), and hamsters (Cricetidae), also hibernate. Physiologically, their hibernation seems similar to that of bats, and where the appropriate experiments have not been done on bats, we will have to extrapolate from our knowledge of these other hibernators.

THE HIBERNACULUM

Since a hibernating animal is defenceless, the choice of a suitable place to spend the winter, the hibernaculum, is crucial. Hibernating rodents generally construct a special nest for the purpose, often in a burrow. Bats are anatomically ill-equipped for nest-building or tunnelling, so instead find natural sites which afford similar shelter: either caves (or such man-made equivalents as mines and cellars, all loosely grouped as 'caves' here), or trees (including crevices in bark and woodpecker holes). Among the British bats, the *Myotis* species, the horseshoe bats *Rhinolophus* and the long-eared bats *Plecotus* are found in caves during the winter. The two *Nyctalus* species, the serotine *Eptesicus serotinus* and *Pipistrellus pipistrellus* are all 'tree' bats, having never (*Nyctalus*) or only rarely been recorded in caves. However, these distinctive habits are not absolutely fixed: *Plecotus* mostly tend to occur in caves before Christmas when these provide a cooler hibernaculum than trees, and in eastern Europe, where winters are more severe, *Nyctalus noctula* and *P. pipistrellus* both regularly take refuge in caves; Krzanowski (1961) recorded catching 27 *E. serotinus* in a Polish cave over five winters. The barbastelle (*B. barbastellus*) seems to be intermediate; it often hibernates through the winter in tree sites, but very severe winter weather drives it into caves. A similar rough division into 'cave bats' and 'tree bats' is found among the American species, but the generic distinctions are not maintained: both *Eptesicus fuscus* and *Pipistrellus subflavus* are cave bats in America, despite the habits of their relatives in Britain.

Caves offer relatively constant conditions, but tree holes generally afford rather less protection from the climate. Heerdt & Sluiter (1965) monitored the temperature inside and outside an empty woodpecker hole, and found that though the inside was buffered from the extreme fluctuations outside, its temperature nevertheless dropped to $-4°C$ when the outside temperature was

−6°C. Bats using such hibernacula often do so in clusters, resulting in considerable metabolic savings. Even so, it is clear that 'tree bats' are, and have to be, much hardier than 'cave bats'.

Probably the hardiest is the red bat (*Lasiurus borealis*), which may roost in the open and get covered with snow. This American species can hibernate despite temperature fluctuations from −5°C up to 20°C, and even withstand parts of its body freezing solid. It has a very well-furred tail membrane, which is wrapped over the ventral surface of the body and almost covers the wings; it is also able to adjust its metabolism very accurately and rapidly in response to experimental changes in ambient temperature. It is presumed to hibernate in trees, since it certainly does not often do so in caves or houses.

Temperatures deep in caves rarely drop below 6°C at the latitudes relevant to hibernating bats, and one might expect all the bats to congregate in such warm regions for the winter. In fact, different species react in different ways. For example, Bezem, Sluiter & Van Heerdt (1964) showed that of the species which hibernated regularly in their study caves in Holland, *Myotis mystacinus, M. nattereri* and *Plecotus auritus* preferred to rest within 50 metres of the entrances, while *M. emarginatus, M. daubentoni* and *Rhinolophus hipposideros* were mostly found deeper than 50 metres. Even within these groups, resting sites differed; *R. hipposideros* always hung free from the ceiling, while *M. daubentoni* invariably tucked itself away in a narrow crevice. *P. auritus* and *M. daubentoni* used horizontal as well as vertical crevices. *M. mystacinus, M. nattereri* and *M. emarginatus* generally stayed vertical.

Nor is it necessarily a constant environment which the cave bats select. It is popularly imagined that hibernating animals remain torpid for long periods of time, even throughout the winter, unless they are disturbed. In fact, many hibernators periodically wake up spontaneously. The bat's ability to arouse seems to depend on having changes of temperature where it is hibernating. The most extensive study of this has been carried out on the greater horseshoe bat, *Rhinolophus ferrumequinum*, by Ransome (1968,

1971). He found that caves in which the temperature varied only slightly (within about 1°C) usually contained very few bats, though at certain restricted times large numbers might be present. Similarly, when he interfered with some cellars in which the bats hibernated, by blocking entrances to restrict the draughts and installing heaters in some of them (both courses of action calculated to reduce the fluctuations in temperature), the numbers of bats present declined sharply and only started to recover when the changes were reversed.

The most striking example reported of the need for variability is in the red bat *Lasiurus borealis*. Although it regularly appears at cave sites during its autumn migration, it does not normally hibernate in them; as we mentioned earlier, this seems to be a 'tree bat'. Occasionally the odd *Lasiurus* seems to get 'trapped' in a cave during the autumn and hibernates there, but it invariably dies, apparently because the temperatures never vary sufficiently to reach levels (about 20°C) which would stimulate it to wake up (Myers, 1960).

Ransome's work has shown that bats not only need variable temperatures in their hibernaculum, but also choose different ambient temperatures through the winter. By taking air temperatures in caves used by hibernating *R. ferrumequinum*, in parts of caves with and without bats, he found that in February the bats were hibernating in an ambient temperature of 4° to 8°C; the previous October, however, they had chosen 8.5° to 12.5°C. This change occurred even though they could have picked a region of constant temperature (in the range 8° to 10°C) which would have taken them through the winter (fig 16); Daan (1973) obtained similar results for three species of *Myotis*. Moreover these changes were not simply due to the region in which the bats had started to hibernate in October becoming colder by March. For example, in one cave which Ransome studied, the region near the entrance had a temperature of about 12°C and up to eighty bats hibernating in it in October each year. By March however, the temperature here was down to 0°C and there were no bats present. On the other hand, the deepest section of the cave contained only one or two bats in October, despite a temperature of 10°C, but by February and March when the temperature was often about 7°C, up to twenty bats were present; evidently they do move around in winter.

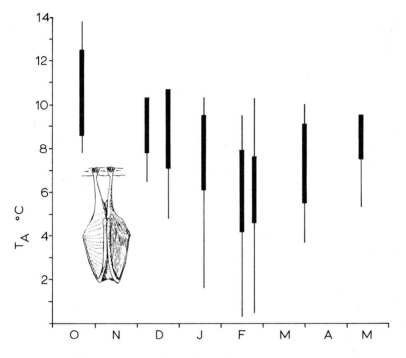

Fig 16. Temperatures available through the winter in caves where greater horseshoe bats (*Rhinolophus ferrumequinum*) were hibernating, showing (thick bands) the temperatures in regions where bats were actually present. (From Ransome, 1968.) The bats are clearly exercising some choice over their surrounding temperatures, but those selected in February are entirely below the range selected in October.

So the temperature regime of the hibernaculum seems to be critical for *R. ferrumequinum*, for the three *Myotis* species and, by implication, for other species too; certainly the variety of species present in a cave often changes during the winter. This poses two questions: can bats select temperatures this accurately, and are other factors of importance during hibernation?

The answer to the first question seems to be yes, though more investigation is needed. Harmata (1969) showed experimentally that the lesser horseshoe, *R. hipposideros*, could select temperatures with an accuracy of 0.8°C, and there are numerous reports of very specific temperature preferences of different species of bats.

The importance of factors other than temperature is less easy to establish. Obviously for a torpid animal, safety from predators is important, but most hibernacula probably meet this requirement anyway. Certainly the deeper regions of caves are fairly safe from all predators except marauding physiologists, though wood-pecker-holes and hollow trees may be less secure. There are some reports of owls taking horseshoe bats from caves, and even tits (*Parus* sp) have been reported killing torpid tree bats, but such events are rare.

Water may be an important factor in the selection of a hiberna-culum for some species; one experimenter is reported to have killed a hibernating *R. hipposideros* in twenty-four hours simply by moving it from a relative humidity of 95 per cent to 80 per cent, and others have observed hibernating bats temporarily wake up, lap drops of condensed moisture from their fur and return to hibernation (Davis, 1970). However, most cave sites are so humid that water loss is not likely to be a problem.

Possibly tree bats experience greater problems with water loss, but there is evidence that they are far more tolerant of it than *Rhinolophus*. This may in part be because *Rhinolophus* hang up to hibernate in such an exposed manner and increase the possibility of water loss by wrapping their wings around themselves like a cloak, whereas most other bats fold their wings away. There are, unfortunately, very few measurements of relative humidity in the neighbourhood of hibernating tree bats, though the atmosphere inside a crowded woodpecker hole could remain very humid for long periods. The only useful information from laboratory work is that the guano bat *Tadarida brasiliensis*, which may hibernate in buildings, can tolerate a relative humidity of only 60 per cent during hibernation at 5°C for anything from 17 to 95 days (quoted by Davis, 1970).

HIBERNATION STRATEGY: FAT RESERVES

We have already noted that hibernating bats metabolise fat. If the fat store has to last the bat through the winter, it must be quite large in the autumn and much depleted by the spring. Many studies indicate that bats can lose anything between 25 and 35 per cent (autumn) weight by the spring. For example, Krzanowski (1961) recorded that male Natterer's bats (*Myotis nattereri*) decline from 9.8g in November to 7.4g in April (26 per cent loss), and females from 12.4g in October to 8.1g in April (36 per cent loss); these were the average weight losses for each sex, and one individual female lost no less than 38 per cent of her October weight over winter.

The difference in weight losses between the sexes is well known and found in all species which have been studied; generally, females lose more over winter than males, but this is because they enter hibernation at higher weights, ie with larger fat reserves. The extraordinary variations in weight lost by different individuals have been investigated, especially for *R. ferrumequinum*, by Ransome (1968); he found that old females entered hibernation on average at 29.2g and lost 34.1 per cent of this over winter, while the old males began hibernating at 24.2g but lost only 24.2 per cent (fig 17). Females need larger reserves to ensure that they can still support a developing foetus (see Chapter 5), despite food shortages, in early spring. The younger adults of both sexes lost slightly more weight than their respective elders, while the juvenile bats of both sexes in their first winter lost about the same proportion of their weight as the adult males (Table 4, page 84). Dissection of a small number of individuals in October confirmed that adult females carried most fat.

Perhaps the most important result from these studies concerns the over-wintering success of the juvenile bats. Fig 15 shows that the smaller juveniles are missing from the spring sample, because

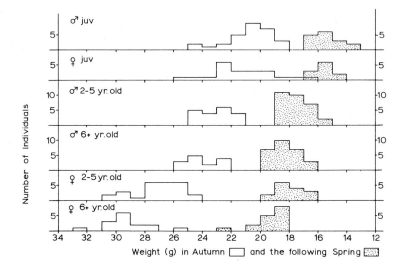

Fig 17. Weights of different age and sex classes of greater horseshoe bats (*Rhinolophus ferrumequinum*) at the beginning and end of hibernation. (From Ransome, 1968.)

juveniles which enter hibernation weighing more than 19.5g have a good chance of survival, while those commencing at lower

TABLE 4

Weight lost over winter by hibernating *Rhinolophus ferrumequinum* (from Ransome, 1968).

Age & sex	Mean weight (g), 12 Oct. 1962 (and sample size)	Mean weight (g), 30 Mar. 1963 (and sample size)	% weight loss
Juv ♂	20·3 (20)	15·3 (16)	24·6
2–5 yr ♂	22·8 (11)	17·1 (30)	25·0
6+ yr ♂	24·2 (9)	18·4 (28)	24·2
Juv ♀	20·9 (13)	15·3 (16)	24·1
2–5 yr ♀	27·7 (15)	18·0 (15)	35·2
6+ yr ♀	29·2 (9)	19·2 (15)	34·1

weights generally die from starvation (Table 5, below). Though the same point has not been proved for other bats, hibernation seems to be equally hazardous for their juveniles. If bats are not born until, say, early July, and not weaned until August, they have only two or three months in which to learn to hunt efficiently enough to lay down fat reserves as well as stay alive. The older bats do not start to accumulate enough fat until the end of September, but when they do start they gain weight very rapidly; Stebbings (1970) reported that *Plecotus austriacus* increased in weight by 16 per cent (9.7 to 11.3g) in a fortnight!

TABLE 5

Survival of juvenile *R. ferrumequinum* (from Ransome, 1968).

Weight	No. entering hibernation 1st winter	No. found 2nd winter	% found 2nd winter
Greater than 19·5 g	46	26	56·5
Less than 19·5 g	19	1	5·3

Ransome's results for *R. ferrumequinum* probably apply to other species too; but the difference in fat reserves and percentage weight loss, especially in adult females as compared to males and juveniles, remain to be explained. Perhaps we should first consider the amount of fat necessary to last a bat through the winter. For the little brown bat, the data from Table 6 will suffice, though the figure we get may not be accurate for other species. This bat weighs about 6g; if it were to hibernate at the temperature ($2°C$) which results in its minimal metabolic rate, it would need 0.0022g of fat daily ($0.03ml\ O_2/g/hr \times 6g \times 24hrs \times 0.0005g$ of fat); if hibernation lasts seven months, then 0.5g of fat should be enough to see the bat through; yet a 30 per cent weight increase would mean 1.8g of fat. *R. ferrumequinum* is a larger species, so should have a marginally lower metabolic rate, but it hibernates at about $9°C$, which would just about double the metabolic rate at

2°C. The similar calculation based on a metabolic rate of 0.07ml O_2/g/hr suggests that a 20g *R. ferrumequinum* might need 4g of fat to see it through a similar period of hibernation, and adult females actually have about 10g. Even the juveniles carry about 5g of fat, so they ought to get by: yet we have seen that in fact many die of starvation.

TABLE 6

Metabolic rates of *Myotis lucifugus* at different ambient temperatures (oxygen consumption from Hock, 1951; other figures from conversion factors below).

T_A °C	Metabolic rate ml O_2/g/hr	Metabolic rate ml CO_2/g/hr	Fat required g/g/hr	Energy released cal/g/hr
0·5	0·113	0·079	0·00006	0·531
2·0	0·030	0·021	0·00002	0·141
10·0	0·071	0·050	0·00004	0·334
20·0	0·393	0·275	0·00020	0·847
30·0	2·00	1·400	0·00102	9·400
37·0	2·89	2·023	0·00147	13·583
41·5	4·14	2·898	0·00211	19·458

Notes: (a) The conversion factors assume a fat-based metabolism. (b) The bat was in hibernation at the lower temperatures. (c) 1 ml O_2 metabolises 0·0005 g of fat, yielding 4·7 calories and 0·7 ml CO_2. (d) 1 g of fat, metabolised by 1·98 1 O_2, yields 9·3 kilocalories and 1·39 1 CO_2.

Hibernating bats can in fact survive periods of 200 days or so under experimental conditions. For instance when Wimsatt wanted to demonstrate that female bats mated in the autumn could conceive the next spring (see Chapter 5), he imprisoned the bats in a refrigerator for 159 days or more; they survived and produced viable embryos the following spring. *Eptesicus fuscus* have been kept hibernating in refrigerators for as long as 344 days before dying of starvation, far longer than would be needed to survive a winter.

Such long survival periods are not possible in the wild simply

Page 87 (above) Natterer's bat, *Myotis nattereri*, bearing a bat ring on its forearm; (*below*) the Holgate Ultrasonic Receiver, a portable bat-detector for field use. The special microphone (left) picks up bats' ultrasonic emissions and these are rendered audible through a loudspeaker built into the detector. A tuning dial (bottom left corner of the instrument) indicates the frequency of the sounds being detected and helps to give some clue to the species of bat present

Page 88 The authors' design of bat grille for protecting small entrances to underground hibernacula. (*Above*) from the inside: a set of horizontal bars slides into reciprocal pipes to eliminate the need for hinges on the gate; (*below*) from the outside: a concrete collar surrounds the installation to protect its edges from damage. The 7 inch gap between the bars allows free passage to bats

because constant conditions are not available. If a bat could settle at a minimum temperature (say 2°C) in October, and stay in that temperature until May, as if in a nicely controlled refrigerator, all would be fine. In practice, if it selects a region of a cave at 2°C in October, by January the temperature will probably be −10°C or —15°C; a region at 2°C in January was probably 15°C or more in October.

Effectively, a bat has two possible strategies. The first is to hibernate deep in caves where the temperature is fairly stable, but much warmer than the temperature at which its metabolic rate would be minimal. For example, eastern pipistrelles (*Pipistrellus subflavus*) hibernate at temperatures of 12° to 13°C in the depths of Kentucky caves and rarely wake up or move (Davis, 1964). This is also the stratagem adopted by the adult female *R. ferrumequinum*. Since the temperatures are rather higher, metabolic rates are also raised and the fat reserves needed are necessarily greater; but we have already seen that adult female *R. ferrumequinum* do indeed have greater fat reserves than males.

The alternative is to try to hibernate in regions where the temperature, and consequent metabolic rate, are lower, but such places are nearer to cave entrances and therefore more affected by variations of winter weather and its increasing severity. As the temperatures fluctuate, the bats must necessarily wake up, and move to a better site. This is what the adult male and juvenile *R. ferrumequinum* do, and so do many bats of other species. The appearance of barbastelles (*Barbastella barbastellus*) in British caves only during very severe weather, for example, indicates movements of this type.

The disadvantage is, of course, that moving about requires a heavy expenditure of energy and fat reserves. In order to warm itself from hibernation at 10°C to activity at 35°C, a small bat would need 450 calories, equivalent to 0.048g of fat, assuming that it was perfectly insulated and lost no heat during this period. This figure is simply derived—a calorie is, by definition, the amount of heat needed to raise the temperature of 1g of water by 1°C.

A 20g bat raising its temperature 25°C might therefore use 500 calories; in fact, its specific heat is about 0.9 (the 20 per cent of its body that is not water warms rather more readily than the amount that is), so giving us the figure of 450 calories. An hour of flight searching for a new hibernating site might require the expenditure of a further 0.29g of fat (using the energy consumption of *Phyllostomus* in flight, 135 calories/g/hr; see Chapter 2). Thus in waking and flying about, it might use up fat equivalent to that consumed in $17\frac{1}{2}$ days of uninterrupted hibernation.

On such approximations, a juvenile *R. ferrumequinum* with only 5g of fat reserves in October could only afford to wake up about four times during a winter. It is clear that hibernating bats, particularly the juveniles, have very little fat to spare. Any disturbance causing extra arousals in midwinter, for instance by cavers or people studying bats, therefore poses a real threat to the bat's survival.

Bats can minimise their metabolic costs by hibernating in cooler places (thus lowering metabolic rate) and clustering together. This may explain the peculiar sex ratios and variable occurrence of clusters which have puzzled workers studying bat populations in winter. It is not unusual to find that a cave population includes 60 per cent males, rather than the 50–50 ratio one would expect; this is particularly true when the caves under study include clusters of bats. On the other hand, small caves, with lower populations of isolated bats, may contain only 30 per cent males. Since males, like juveniles, have lower fat reserves, they have to conserve their fat reserves more than the females. By gathering into clusters, they iron out minor fluctuations in cave temperature, contribute their own microclimate and may reduce their individual heat loss by reducing their total exposed surface area.

AROUSAL AND FEEDING

So far we have made the major assumption that bats enter hibernation with their fat deposits fully formed and 'rely' on those reserves to last them throughout the winter; we have presupposed that no feeding occurs during hibernation, and that the bats do not wake up unless temperature fluctuations or disturbance force them to move. There is increasing evidence that these assumptions are not necessarily true. For example, Krzanowski (1961) recorded many instances where individually marked bats, weighed during hibernation, showed gains in weight on successive occasions, strongly suggesting that they had been out feeding. One male *Myotis daubentoni* increased 20 per cent in weight in eleven days (from 6.91g on 28 January 1957, to 8.34g· on 8 February). While some of the smaller gains might have resulted from drinking, large increases of this sort surely indicate feeding. Conclusive evidence of feeding during hibernation has come from Ransome's studies of greater horseshoes. Fresh droppings were found on cave floors during every winter month in one year or another, and occasionally some fresh beetle remains.

Ransome also discovered that at least the juveniles rarely hibernated for more than ten days at a time and usually for only about six days. When outside temperatures were 10–11°C, the bats woke up every night, presumably flying out to feed when possible. When the temperature was down to 7°C, they were likely to spend about six days in uninterrupted hibernation. Interestingly enough, by late winter they were arousing every day with outside temperatures of 8° to 9°C, and needing temperatures of 5°C to keep them in hibernation as long as six days. This tendency to wake up during warmer weather only makes sense if there are food insects available, which seems unlikely in midwinter; but a leading entomologist, C. B. Williams, has sampled nocturnal insects in Britain over many years and his results show that they are still numerous at least until November. From December through to April numbers are low, but even in January, for example, he caught 300 flies per month in Scotland (fig 18). Even more important, from the bat's point of view, is the fact that the winter catch varied enormously; on a warm night in January, as many insects were caught as on average nights in September and October (Williams, 1939, 1961). Obviously, if bats take advantage of such warm nights, they can compensate for the loss of fat reserves incurred through waking up and flying about.

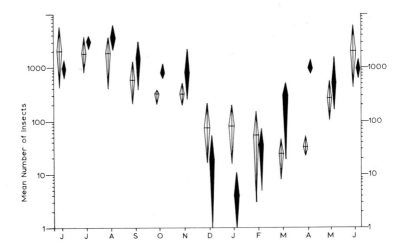

Fig 18.   Insect availability through the year. Open symbols show the number of insects caught in a light trap per night (at Rothamsted, Hertfordshire, SE England). Closed symbols show number of moths caught per month (at Kincraig, Perthshire, Scotland). Each diamond shows the mean of four year's results and the range. During a mild January in the south of England there may be as many insects flying as in October or November, but catches are low in April. In Scotland, catches are low in December-January, but begin to improve in April. (Based on Williams, 1939 & 1961.)

Thus we have a further modification of the strategies that hibernating bats can follow. They could retreat deep into caves, where temperatures are rather warm, but stable. They may remain near the cave entrance, perhaps settling in a colder temperature to minimise metabolism, but in a variable temperature zone so that if the outside temperature warms up they are awakened and fly out at dusk to feed. Obviously in practice all possible intermediates and combinations of these are likely. Juvenile bats in particular are likely to remain active into November, feeding whenever possible. We might expect that those bats which wake up to feed lose less weight (especially in a mild or erratic winter) than those which retreat deep into a cave. Ransome has in fact shown this to be true for *R. ferrumequinum*. The adult females lose weight at a steady rate of 0.0024 grammes of fat per gramme of body weight per day, but juveniles and males show very erratic rates of loss, rather higher than the adult females in December–February, but very much lower in November (fig 19).

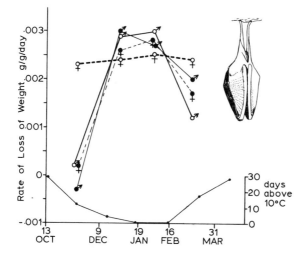

Fig 19.   Rate of loss of weight in the different age-sex categories of greater horseshoe bat (*Rhinolophus ferrumequinum*), in grammes per gramme body weight per day. Adult females lose weight at a steady rate, the others lose weight erratically, because they hunt whenever possible. Insects are likely to be flying at night if daytime temperatures exceed 10°C; the number of days each month on which this happened are indicated along the bottom. (Based on Ransome, 1968.)

Clearly, these low rates of loss are due to successful feeding. Incidentally, we may note that the adult females' actual rate of weight loss, 0.0024 grammes per gramme of body weight per day, or 0.0001g per hour, is 2½ times the rate we used in our calculations on p 86! This discrepancy is in part due to water loss, not considered there, and partly due to the errors implicit in basing our calculations on a different species (*Myotis lucifugus*). Bats which have been out feeding have to maintain their body temperatures while digesting the food, and will of course need to minimise their heat losses during this period, since any digested food not wasted as heat can be stored as fat. This provides another powerful incentive to form clusters which, as we have already noted, are most likely in *R. ferrumequinum* to be formed by those age-sex groups which indulge in winter feeding.

BEGINNING AND END OF HIBERNATION

Causes of Arousal

We have noted that both declining temperatures (approaching freezing point) and rising temperatures (nearing perhaps 10°C when insects might be available) can arouse bats from hibernation. Physical disturbance, such as handling, also causes awakening. In addition, Ransome's (1971) results show that even undisturbed bats may wake up spontaneously after a few days. It has been demonstrated by Menaker (1959) for little brown bats (*Myotis lucifugus*), and by Pohl (1961) for mouse-eared (*M. myotis*), that even bats hibernating in a constant environment may show daily cycles in their metabolism—body temperatures and respiratory rates showed slight but regular increases towards evening. A similar circadian rhythm is likely in other species and could of course trigger arousal at the appropriate time for feeding. Arousal at the end of hibernation could be triggered by accumulation of metabolites such as urea, which can cause arousal when injected into hibernating animals. A switch from fat metabolism to protein metabolism as the fat reserves run out has also been suggested as a trigger. The most likely stimulus still seems to be the increasing ambient temperature, felt by any bat hibernating in a moderately exposed site as spring arrives, a suggestion supported by reports of individual *Pipistrellus subflavus* and *Myotis emarginatus* (two species which hibernate deep in the stable region of caves) still soundly hibernating in mid-June. The unfortunate *Lasiurus* which get themselves 'stuck' in caves should also be remembered in this connection.

Mechanisms of Arousal

We saw earlier that to arouse itself might cost an individual *R. ferrumequinum* 450 calories. The rapidity with which this heat is released is remarkable, for a bat can warm up enough to be able to fly in about 60 minutes. Smaller bats arouse faster still; little brown bats may need only 30 minutes. Five possible heat sources deserve consideration:

1. Heart muscle. The first sign in the animal's metabolism that arousal has commenced is a sharp increase in the heart rate, followed by an increase in the respiration rate. The heart will produce some heat, particularly during the early stages of arousal when it is 'racing' against low blood pressure. However, the heart is less than 1 per cent of the body weight, say 0.2g in a 20g bat; even at the metabolic rate of flight muscle during flying it would only produce about 16 calories during the hour's warm-up (assuming 20 per cent of its work appears as pumping and 80 per cent as heat).

2. Other viscera. It is not known how much the metabolism of the liver, for example, might contribute to the warming-up process, but it is known that eviscerated hamsters can arouse satisfactorily. It is also known, in hamsters, that the blood supply to the posterior half of the body is restricted during warming up, so that at the mid-point in the process the hindquarters may be 10°C colder than the front (Lyman & Chatfield, 1950). These factors probably apply also to bats and indicate that the viscera are not important to arousal (Rauch & Hayward, 1970).

3. External heat. When available this is an important factor in arousal. For instance, arousal in an ambient temperature of 25°C takes roughly half as long as arousal from 5°C. However, there is

no doubt that bats, and other hibernators, can and do arouse from low temperatures despite lack of external heat. We have already defined hibernation as including the ability to do this.

4. Body musculature. This is certainly important during normal arousal from hibernation. Shivering can be recorded electronically and reaches a peak when the body temperature is between 15°C and 20°C. However, during the first twenty to thirty minutes of arousal at an ambient temperature of 5°C, no shivering occurs (Mejsnar & Jansky, 1970); moreover, the drug curare can be used to paralyse the skeletal musculature without inhibiting arousal from these low temperatures (Lyman & Chatfield, 1950). In other words, shivering is an important source of heat during the middle part of the warming-up process, but not initially essential.

5. Brown fat. This interesting tissue occurs as a large deposit between the scapulae in hibernators, earning it the speculative name 'hibernating gland', but it is not confined to hibernators, being found widely in young mammals (including humans). Histologically it seems well equipped for rapid heat-production, for its cells contain many very large mitochondria (the cell 'power houses' containing the enzymes of oxidation). It is possible to knock out brown-fat metabolism with the drug hexamethonium; when this is done with bats trying to arouse from 5°C they completely fail to warm up. On the other hand, bats arousing at 25°C warm up quite well, though they do take somewhat longer than when brown-fat metabolism can assist. Mejsnar and Jansky suggested that brown-fat metabolism may contribute about 25 per cent of the heat production at either end of the warming-up process, but only about 10 per cent in the middle when shivering is more important. Brown fat produces the heat to raise the body temperature to the point where the muscles can begin shivering.

So shivering and brown-fat metabolism are the two major heat sources for the warming process. It has been known for some time that arousal includes two stages, a slow first half and a much more rapid second phase. We can now suggest that the slow first half represents brown-fat heat production and the faster second phase represents shivering thermogenesis, or a combination of the two.

Entry into Hibernation

Inducing a bat to enter hibernation is much more difficult than studying its arousal processes, so that much less is known about the onset of hibernation. Basically there are two theories, one that the bat 'shuts off' its temperature-control mechanism and therefore 'falls' into hibernation. The other supposes that it slows down its metabolism, meaning it cannot keep up its temperature. Certainly it does not actively cool itself. The few measurements that have been made suggest that the heart-rate of a bat exposed to cold at first increases, as the bat tries to keep up its temperature, but then starts to fluctuate cyclically, finally continuing to drop from one of the low points in the cycle. This rather suggests that in fact it slows down its metabolism and cools as a result.

The more distant factors which precipitate hibernation are equally uncertain. In bats, and in other hibernators, falling temperature, lack of food, hormone balance and adequate fat deposits are all involved, but which of these is paramount, or whether any of them alone is enough to cause entry into hibernation, remains in doubt.

THE EVOLUTION OF HIBERNATION

So far, we have discussed hibernation as an overwintering phenomenon of insectivorous Microchiroptera in temperate climates, and we have also mentioned some tropical bats which are homeotherms. This might suggest a complete dichotomy among bats; but, as so often in zoology, the boundaries between these two extremes are much obscured by intermediate levels of temperature regulation. Before we can profitably discuss the evolution of hibernation, we must consider the phenomenon of daily torpor, a subject well known to many naturalists. Bats which enter hibernation in winter are usually found to be torpid during the daytime in summer as well. Are daily torpidity in summer and hibernation in winter simply the same physiological mechanism?

If one catches, say, *Myotis lucifugus*, which hibernate perfectly well in winter, in July and subject them to ambient temperatures below 7°C, they become hypothermic and unable to arouse themselves, though in winter they can arouse themselves perfectly well from even lower temperatures (Menaker, 1962). However, if they are first acclimatised in a refrigerator for three weeks they regain their ability to arouse from the cold. This same phenomenon has been reported for *M. myotis* and *Eptesicus fuscus*, and is presumably widespread. It emphasises that there are differences between daily torpor and hibernation. Possibly summer bats lack an appropriate store of brown fat, though this has not yet been investigated; nor has the fact that torpid summer bats wake up to feed most evenings, while hibernating bats may pass many days without waking.

Daily torpor, or at least the ability to become torpid, is common among bats of temperate latitudes. There is increasing evidence that species which in the laboratory enter daily torpor do not necessarily do so under natural conditions. They may instead roost in places where the sun's warmth is particularly effective and they may also resort to clustering. Bats of other families may indulge in daily torpor, perhaps the source of controversy over whether certain species do or do not hibernate. *Tadarida brasiliensis*, for example, is said by Herreid (1967) to hibernate, but Lyman (1970) seems to consider no molossid to be a deep hibernator, regarding this presumably as an example of daily torpidity. (Many humming-birds also show daily torpor, though none are known to hibernate.)

Torpidity, like hibernation, seems to be a means of conserving energy, enabling insectivorous bats to inhabit latitudes where the food supply is too erratic to maintain activity the whole time.

THERMOREGULATION IN TROPICAL BATS

Large tropical bats are perfectly good homeotherms. Even though, in the wild, they would probably not experience temperatures as low as 5°C, when confronted with these in the laboratory they are able to step up their metabolism and maintain their normal body temperature.

Small tropical bats present a more confused picture. Some evidently try to maintain their body temperature and are successful in relatively cool conditions, but cannot cope with severe cold. For example, the small fruit bat *Syconycteris australis* (18g) was unable to maintain its body temperature at an ambient temperature of 5°C, despite a 500 per cent increase in metabolic rate. Other species appear to relax their degree of regulation in the middle range of ambient temperatures, but maintain body heat at both high and low ambient temperatures (eg *Rhinopoma* and *Leptonycteris*). Others, particularly the very small species, seem unable to compensate for low air temperatures (eg *Natalus*).

Much of this information has been clarified by McNab (1969). The ability of a mammal to keep warm depends upon the balance between its heat-producing mechanism (its metabolism), and its efficiency at conserving the heat produced (its insulation). McNab measured the oxygen consumption of numerous species of tropical bats at different ambient temperatures in order to find their basal metabolic rate. He found that fruit, nectar and meat-eating bats had generally higher metabolic rates than other mammals of comparable size. On the other hand, insectivorous bats and vampires had relatively low basal metabolic rates. Having recorded the body temperatures of his bats, McNab could work out the conductances (a measure of the rate of heat loss; the reciprocal of insulation). Not surprisingly, in view of their large surface areas, all bats tended to have rather higher conductances than other mammals of comparable size (fig 20).

So fruit and nectar feeding bats are able to balance their high conductances by their higher rate of heat production, and so maintain their body temperatures. Insectivorous species, with lower rates of basal metabolism, do not have the necessary spare heat-producing capacity and therefore fall into torpor when the ambient temperature is lowered. McNab suggested that the fruit bats have plentiful food supplies, rich in calories, and therefore can as it were afford these high metabolic rates; insectivorous bats, even in the tropics, may face seasonal shortages which

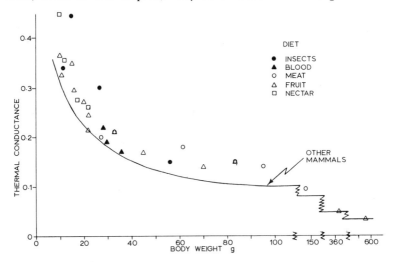

Fig 20.   The rate of heat loss expressed as an index of thermal conductance (the reciprocal of insulation) plotted against body size in bats. All bats, except the very largest, lose heat faster than other mammals of comparable size and are therefore more vulnerable to cold (after McNab, 1969).

necessitate a more economical metabolic rate and the ability to lapse into torpor. Insect food may also be less nutritious, weight for weight, and the energy expenditure necessary to catch it may leave less 'spare'. The somewhat poor performance of the vampires seems strange, but before the Spanish conquest and the advent of horses and cattle in South America, vampires too may have been periodically short of food.

The ability of tropical insectivorous bats to enter periodic torpidity was a useful preadaptation for the invasion of temperate regions, and may well have been the physiological base from which long-term hibernation evolved.

THE ORIGIN OF HIBERNATION

Many physiologists have regarded the daily torpidity and winter hibernation of mammals as a primitive character retained from their cold-blooded reptilian ancestors. We have seen that this is nonsense; reptiles are unable to control their body temperatures when placed in a low ambient temperature, whereas a hibernating bat is quite capable of increasing its metabolic rate if the temperature gets too near freezing. We have also seen that daily torpidity and seasonal hibernation are physiologically rather different mechanisms, though the tolerance of the brain to low temperatures, for example, is probably an attribute common to both.

If the torpidity shown by tropical insectivorous bats preadapted them to the exploitation of seasonally abundant insect food in temperate latitudes, this is in accord with the idea that bats were, primarily and primitively, a tropical group, of which some members have succeeded in spreading to temperate climes. Why then do they not migrate back to the tropics each winter as birds do? Three possibilities present themselves.

Bats usually fly at much slower speeds than birds. Probably their hunting success depends in part on this, but when it comes to migrating it is likely to be a serious disadvantage, for the ability to make progress against a headwind depends on the excess of one's flightspeed over the windspeed. Clearly a migrator must expect to meet headwinds on some occasions, no matter how carefully departure is timed to coincide with tail winds. It may be relevant here that some of the fastest-flying bats (eg *Tadarida* and *Lasiurus*) are among the few which do undertake very long migrations.

If catching insects in flight is a strenuous method of obtaining food and leaves little to spare for storage as fat, bats might have difficulty laying down enough fat reserves to support a long migration. It is true, of course, that swifts and swallows manage to do this, also that bats have to lay down fat reserves anyway in order to hibernate. But a slow-flying bat like the greater horseshoe, probably travelling at about 5 metres per second, a mere 18km per hour, would fly for about 194 hours in order to migrate the 3,500km from England to West Africa; if it could not feed en route, it might need a fat reserve of about 70g. (This figure is an extrapolation from data of Thomas & Suthers, 1972 relating to *Phyllostomus*, not an aerodynamically efficient species; but even if it were as efficient in flight as *Rousettus*, it would still need about 17g of fat.) It is obviously better off contenting itself with the 10g necessary to see it through hibernation.

Also, ecologically speaking, it may be advantageous to hibernate through very cold weather and exploit the temporary abundance of insects which fly on warm nights. The migratory birds which would consume these (such as swallows and martins) leave by mid-October. Were they to remain, they would risk being caught by a cold snap; hibernating bats are well equipped to survive these, but migratory birds are not.

Finally, why can wrens, which are insectivorous, remain active when bats have to hibernate? The answer here is largely that bats rely on catching flying insects, which in turn require a reasonably high temperature before they can fly. Wrens feed amongst leaf litter, under bushes, etc, where they can pick off stationary insects, spiders and other small terrestrial invertebrates. Even so, wrens do sometimes suffer severe winter mortality; the 1962–3 winter killed something like 90 per cent of those in southern England.

CHAPTER 5

REPRODUCTION AND GROUP BEHAVIOUR

The reproduction cycles of bats often include interesting, even unique, features, especially where modifications have arisen because the breeding cycle is interrupted by some other major event such as hibernation. Each species may have its own special annual cycle and may even vary it from place to place, though temperate-zone hibernators are basically similar, and the greatest variability occurs in tropical species. From the wealth of diverse but frequently incomplete information, it is difficult to generalise accurately: it would also be confusing to enunciate every detail. In this review of bat reproductive patterns, particular attention is paid to interesting deviations from the mammalian norm.

Too often we know only part of the story; for instance, certain bats have been studied intensively when they congregate to hibernate or to breed, but little is known about them at other times of year, when dispersed. With tropical species, short-term expeditions have collected specimens, plucking out a sample of the bat's life cycle, but we are unable to relate this to what went before or after. Only recently have regular year-round studies been completed, even on quite common bats, and still we have much to learn regarding modifications of breeding cycles forced upon bats by climatic variations in different parts of their range.

The fascinating 'special case' of *Miniopterus* is an example discussed later, but it surely cannot be unique?

MATERNAL COLONIES

Some Megachiroptera have quite elaborate courtship rituals, and *Hypsignathus* is said to indulge in 'lekking' behaviour rather like that seen in black grouse and birds of paradise. For most species of bat, courtship is perfunctory at best and mating appears promiscuous and unselective. The pair-bond seems to be ephemeral and in most species, once separate, the individual males and females usually meet again only accidentally, if at all.

In many bats, perhaps most, the sexes separate before parturition. The expectant mothers, sometimes accompanied by a few immature males, move to a special (often traditional) place to form a nursing colony. In guano bats (*Tadarida brasiliensis*) many of the males seem to stay in Mexico, living up to 1,000 miles from the females and young. The purpose of sex segregation is not clear, though as the males take no part in rearing the young they may be better off out of the way. With the larger nursing colonies, the absence of thousands of males reduces confusion and also reduces competition for food when the mothers need it most, and when the newly weaned young start seeking it for themselves. These nursing colonies vary in size from clusters of half a dozen individuals to the 4 million fruit bats which smother the trees at Cape York in Australia. The biggest bat colony known is in Bracken Cave at San Antonio, Texas, where 20 million guano bats assemble after their long migration from Mexico to form the largest single aggregation of mammals in the world. Within the bat colonies, individuals may huddle closely together in solid masses or they may space themselves out, depending upon species, but we know little of the behaviour of individuals, partly due to the difficulty of making accurate observations among a constantly moving mass, in the dark.

Each species tends to choose a particular type of site to house the nursing colony. Fruit bat colonies usually hang among the branches of a shady tree; various Microchiroptera choose retreats in caves, drainage culverts and the cool, airy ruins of historic monuments such as ancient tombs and Roman amphitheatres. Some habitual tree-dwelling bats, like noctules (*Nyctalus noctula*), will seek hollow trees and woodpecker holes, often competing with hole-nesting birds. Others, such as the serotine (*Eptesicus serotinus*), use house roofs, as will some species like the little brown bat (*Myotis lucifugus*) that have spent the previous winter in a cave. Attics may sometimes become stiflingly hot during the summer, but this may be advantageous to the young, hairless bats. Investigators have recorded air temperatures of 55°C (131°F) among a roof-dwelling colony of *M. lucifugus,* and one of us has watched free-tailed bats (*Molossus ater*) in Trinidad leaving houses whose corrugated-iron roofs are mercilessly cooked by the tropical sun until the metal is far too hot to touch and the atmosphere in the attic, with its tropical humidity, becomes intolerable to the human visitor.

BREEDING SEASONS

Factors which trigger breeding seasons in mammals include changes in light (increasing or decreasing daylength), rainfall and temperature. All species of bats in temperate regions are monoestrous, that is to say they have only one reproductive period per year and produce a single litter each time (Table 7).

TABLE 7

Generalisations on chiropteran oestrous cycles.

Monoestrous: Rhinopomatidae; Megadermatidae; Rhinolophidae.

Generally polyoestrous: Noctilionidae; Nycteridae; Phyllostomidae; Desmodontidae.

Some species monoestrous, some polyoestrous: Pteropodidae; Vespertilionidae; Molossidae.

Probably monoestrous and cyclic: most Australian and Holarctic species (ie bats in high latitudes).

Mostly polyoestrous, non-seasonal breeders: most tropical American bats.

In the tropics, daylength and temperatures are relatively constant and some of the bats in these areas will breed in all months, though probably producing still only one litter per year. With vampires (*Desmodus*) for example, fertile males are always present, and as the females are polyoestrous (have repeated oestrous cycles, one after another) they can be found pregnant at any time, so that juveniles of various ages are present in the population all the year round.

Some tropical bats have a more restricted breeding season, with the annual cycle geared to seasonal changes in rainfall. The young are produced to coincide with plant flowering or fruiting seasons, or with the time of maximal insect abundance.

DELAYED FERTILISATION AND DEVELOPMENT

The temperate-zone species usually hibernate, and ideally the development of the young should commence *immediately* this ends, so as to allow them the longest possible period of growth before the onset of the next winter. But since the reproductive systems of adult bats are quiescent during hibernation, and body reserves depleted at its end, there is bound to be a 'waiting period' whilst the process of sperm production gets under way in the male.

There are three possible solutions to this problem. Assuming that spermatogenesis occurs in summer when the males are in peak condition, and ceases during the autumn and winter: 1, viable sperm could be stored within the male bat, ready to fertilise females as soon as hibernation ends; or 2, after mating, sperm could be stored in the female but not fertilise the ova until the spring (delayed fertilisation); or 3, mating and fertilisation could occur before winter, but the implantation and/or development of the embryo could be arrested until the spring (delayed development).

The bats show examples of each of these phenomena. Sperm storage within the male is certainly possible. After spermatogenesis ceases in late summer, the testes regress but the sperm remain fully viable for up to seven months (Racey, 1973). This is quite long enough to ensure that fertile matings are possible as soon as hibernation ends, or even during brief periods of winter activity. Sperm storage is a special ability of bats; in other mammals, sperm retained in the male reproductive tract begins to lose its viability after only three weeks. Bats have a low reproductive rate and the ability to store sperm over winter may have the additional advantage of enabling males to inseminate yearling females, too young to have ovulated the previous autumn.

The bats may mate at any time in the autumn or during the periods of wakefulness which punctuate hibernation, but the females are not fertile at this time. They do not ovulate until the spring, so that fertilisation of the ovum is postponed until after hibernation has ended. Delayed fertilisation is a variant on the normal patterns of mammalian reproduction which is unique to bats (fig 21). Sperm are stored in the female tract in a semi-liquid mass. Here they remain over winter, dormant but fully viable. If the mass is extracted and dissolved in saline solution, the sperm quickly regain their full motility, but then do not survive for long.

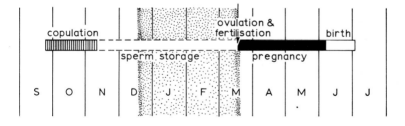

Fig 21. Delayed fertilisation. In the normal pattern of mammalian reproduction, the egg is fertilised soon after mating and pregnancy begins immediately. In many bats, mating occurs in late summer and early autumn, but sperm remain dormant in the female over winter and fertilisation does not take place until the spring.

The exact mechanism which enables the life of stored sperm to be extended from a few hours to several months is not understood: it has been suggested that carbon dioxide may accumulate in the uterus and effectively narcotise the sperm, or that during hibernation the lowered body temperature of the female reduces the metabolic activity of the sperm, causing them to 'hibernate' too. Against this is the fact that bats do not hibernate continuously and may briefly become fully active during the winter. Either way, the female must supply additional nutrient material to the sperm to keep them alive for these long periods, for they do not have energy stores of their own. Racey and Potts (1970) used histochemical techniques to show that the uterine wall actually secretes a substance which may serve to nourish the sperm during the winter. As if to aid this refuelling operation, all the sperm line up and face towards the secretory lining of the uterus.

Meanwhile, inside the ovary, the progress of the Graafian follicle containing the ripening ovum is also arrested for the winter, and there may be some special energy source within the follicle to maintain it during the months of hibernation. Experiments with captive noctule bats indicate that fertilisation can be delayed for $6\frac{1}{2}$ months after mating; in captive pipistrelles, sperm remained viable within the female for five months (Racey, 1973), and the interval exceeds five months in wild *Eptesicus fuscus* and *Myotis lucifugus*, spanning their periods of hibernation. Though the ability to keep sperm viable over winter is obviously advantageous to species which hibernate, neither hypothermia nor daily torpor are essential for the mechanism to work. Tropical vespertilionids (*Tylonycteris pachypus*, *T. robustula*) have also proved capable of prolonged sperm storage, despite their normally high and constant body temperature. Moreover, Racey's captive noctules showed prolonged sperm storage in both sexes even though they were fed and remained active all winter.

Although the existence of delayed fertilisation in bats has been known for a hundred years, there is much to be learned concerning the biochemical details; studies may well prove valuable to human affairs, for there is considerable economic interest in the subject of live sperm storage for artificial insemination of domestic animals, for the breeding of endangered species and for vasectomised men.

The female bats ovulate in the spring after emerging from hibernation and fertilisation of the ovum then takes place, leading to normal foetal development. The trigger which 'switches on' the arrested reproductive processes in the female bat may coincide with a migration from the winter roost to a breeding colony, and is probably associated with increased ambient temperatures and food supplies affecting the bat's hormonal balance, by way of the brain and pituitary gland.

Another peculiar variant on the standard mammalian reproductive cycle is that of delayed development. Here the egg is fertilised normally and develops to the blastocyst stage, but no further. The blastocyst remains in the uterine lumen until some hormonal influence, triggered by environmental factors, prepares the uterine wall to form a functional placenta and permits normal foetal development to proceed. Functionally, delayed development serves to extend the gestation period, so that the young are born at the best time of year. It is well known in temperate mammals like the European badger, stoat, grey seal and roe deer; it is unexpected in an equatorial species, yet apparently occurs in the fruit bat *Eidolon helvum* (Mutere, 1967) living on the equator in Uganda.

In the case of *Eidolon*, mating occurs in early summer, but development of the dormant blastocyst coincides with the peak of the autumnal rainy season, so that the bat foetus develops at the same time as the local vegetation and is born at a time of abundant food. The foetal development time of four months thus follows a three-to-five-month period of delayed development, making seven to nine months in total (perhaps the longest gestation period for any bat). Delayed development is suspected in the North American phyllostomid *Macrotus californicus*, though it is yet to be proved that development is truly arrested in this species. It may just be subject to a long period of very sluggish progress during the early period of foetal growth, as seen in another phyllostomid, *Artibeus jamaicensis*. In this species two early litters develop normally, but ova fertilised in late summer (after the second litter) remain as implanted but dormant blastocysts for two and a half months before completing their development at the normal rate (Fleming, 1971).

An interesting case is that of the long-fingered bat, *Miniopterus schreibersi*, whose breeding cycle is geared to latitude. The genus is essentially tropical in its distribution, occurring mainly in the warmer parts of Africa and Asia, where fertilisation is immediately followed by normal foetal development. The species also ranges beyond the tropics into southern Europe, where it has to hibernate for part of the year. However, although this major physiological event is inserted into its annual cycle, the long-fingered bat retains its tropical reproductive pattern and has not evolved the specialised mechanism of delayed fertilisation seen in true temperate-zone bats. The male cycle does not overlap the hibernation period at all; the testes regress and sperm are not retained over winter in the manner of other hibernating bats. Mating takes place in August and September and the females have to hibernate whilst pregnant. Delayed development occurs, so that the fertilised egg does not grow beyond the blastocyst stage until the end of winter.

Two species of *Miniopterus* (*M. schreibersi* and *M. australis*) also range into the temperate zone of the southern hemisphere, as far as latitude 30°S in Australia. Here there is a similar retardation of embryonic development, but at lower latitudes where the bats do not hibernate gestation is correspondingly shorter (Wimsatt, 1969a). In all cases the net effect is to ensure that the young are produced at the most favourable time of year (fig 22). This variation of reproductive patterns according to latitude is apparently unique among the Chiroptera, but no other species of bat inhabits such a wide range of climatic regions. Commensurate with this, *Miniopterus* also has a wide altitudinal range (we have found these bats at 2,000ft and 11,000ft in Ethiopia; the true extremes are probably even greater) and it would be interesting to know whether altitude also influences the breeding cycle in this genus.

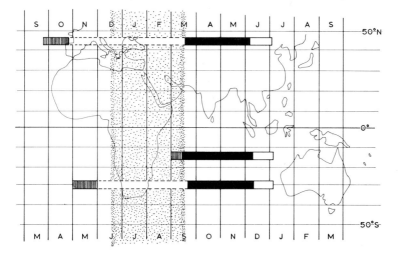

Fig 22.   Breeding seasons in the long-fingered bat (*Miniopterus schreibersi*). At 15°S the copulation period (vertical bars) is followed directly by ovulation and pregnancy (black). Births (white) occur about three months later. At higher latitudes, both N and S of the equator, implantation does not follow immediately after copulation; instead, development is delayed over the winter period (stippled shading), resulting in births in early summer. (After various authors.)

DEVELOPMENT

Once the fertilised egg has implanted, its development in bats is still slow compared with other mammals. In pipistrelles, for instance, it takes over forty-four days to produce one young. (The pigmy shrew, of comparable size, produces litters of up to eight young in only three weeks.) The vampire foetus seems to take over five months to develop, perhaps as long as eight months, and a similarly extended gestation is also described for *Macrotus californicus* (Bradshaw, 1962). Post-implantation development averages

111

two to three months among British vespertilionids and the young are typically born around the end of June.

Long gestation periods are effectively lengthened still further by the phenomenon of delayed fertilisation and with bats of temperate regions there is yet another complication. Foetal development rates are affected by temperature and food supply, and in species that become torpid in the daytime, or during periods of inclement weather, embryonic development is further retarded. Experimenting with captive pregnant pipistrelles made torpid by being kept in a refrigerator, Racey (1969) found that gestation could be artificially extended by a time equivalent to the period of induced torpor. If embryonic development is similarly retarded in the wild by environmental factors, a lengthened and highly variable gestation period will be observed—from a minimum of 56 to a maximum of 100 days has been reported within a single species (*Plecotus rafinesquii*). The concept of a fixed gestation period in bats seems to be inappropriate.

Most bats produce one offspring per season; multiple births only occur regularly in four families, and in only one (Vespertilionidae) are three or more young per litter ever found. The sole genus in which family size frequently exceeds two is *Lasiurus*, which often has twins or triplets, and even quadruplets. The female *Lasiurus* has an extra pair of mammae to cope with the additional demands. There was a recent report (Hamilton & Stalling, 1972) of two of these female red bats being found, each with five young clinging to it; it is possible that they were fostering young from other parents. Among British bats, single young are produced as a rule, although in continental Europe the same species may regularly bear twins. For example in the Netherlands, at least 20 per cent of female noctules give birth to twins (Sluiter & van Heerdt, 1966), and triplets have been recorded. Because of their generally small litter size, bat populations have a very slow intrinsic rate of increase, perhaps compensated for by their unusually long lifespans (Chapter 6).

The bat foetus is very large, sometimes reaching nearly one-third the weight of its mother. This is a heavy burden for the female to carry (imagine a 40lb human foetus!) especially in flight, and birth is a stressful event only rarely witnessed.

Most mothers give birth during the daytime, sometimes using their teeth or one foot to help. Kleiman (1969) was able to watch several births among her captive noctules, and noted that the expectant mother would first turn round from her normal roosting posture, so as to face upwards, then curl the interfemoral membrane under her body forming a pouch to catch the infant bat. Delivery took fifteen to twenty minutes, with the mother frequently licking the baby as it emerged head first. It squeaked frequently during this process and continued to do so after birth as it scrambled vigorously over the mother's fur before attaching itself under her wing. The females continued to groom their young frequently, including spreading and licking the wings. There seemed to be a strong feeling for the baby at first; the mother would show great agitation if separated from it and she would retrieve it as quickly as possible.

In the noctule and most other species studied, the young are not cared for indiscriminately, but specifically by their own mother. As in large colonies of seals or birds, there must be some kind of individual recognition, apparently by audible signals and olfactory cues. When alone, the young emit 'isolation calls', partly ultrasonic and longer in duration than echolocation pulses. The female is attracted by the sound and often replies; then she approaches closely to check the baby's identity by smelling it. Scent glands are well developed in the Chiroptera, smell being the best method for specific recognition of individuals, especially in the darkness of typical bat haunts. Often the maternal bond is completely exclusive, the female nursing only her own offspring and rejecting advances by others, though by the time the babies are about three weeks old and nearly weaned, this bond is considerably weakened. Parental care by male bats is unknown.

It is reported that the mother carries her new-born young when she flies out to feed at night. Females have often been seen, and photographed, carrying young (fig 23), but perhaps these bats had been disturbed and forced to fly carrying the baby. Taking the young on long feeding flights would be unnecessarily arduous and could not be done for long owing to the baby's increasing size.

Fig 23. A young bat carried by its mother (from a photograph of the serotine, *Eptesicus serotinus*).

The young bats of the colony are usually left in a crèche; huddling together may help them to keep warm, especially before their pelage develops, and the choice of a sun-warmed hollow tree or stuffy attic for the site of a nursing colony may also help. Possibly the young of solitary species, lacking warm neighbours, are able to become torpid and withstand hypothermia like the nestlings of the swift.

GROWING UP

Most Microchiroptera are born pink and naked, but the skin becomes pigmented quite soon, sometimes within hours, and the juvenile pelage begins to grow in a few days. Usually the eyes are closed at birth (though in Megachiroptera the young are often well furred and have their eyes open). The ears are floppy and droop over the face, but become erect at about the same time as the eyes open. The mouth and feet are disproportionately large in young bats, the latter almost three-quarters adult size: they are functionally important even in the earliest stages of life, for the baby needs to cling tightly to its mother or to the roost wall. If it falls off it may well be abandoned. By contrast, the wings are not used for some weeks and are small and stubby at birth, retaining a diminutive, screwed-up appearance until the juvenile begins to fly, when they develop rapidly and reach adult proportions within two or three months.

In many mammals (humans for example), the teeth do not need to erupt until some time after birth, but in young bats teeth help to cling to mother, even when she is in flight. The jaws and milk teeth are well developed at birth; a newborn *Myotis lucifugus* already has twenty teeth and baby noctules begin life with all twenty-two milk teeth present, their replacement by the permanent dentition beginning on the thirteenth day after birth and ending sometime during the weaning period. In most families the young cling direct to the mother's fur, but the female rhinolophids and hipposiderids have two false nipples, one on each side of the abdomen. They have no associated glandular tissue and thus do not yield milk: their sole function is to act as 'dummies' for the infant to suck and hang on to.

Young bats squeak lustily, especially when left behind by the mother. These 'isolation calls' have an ultrasonic component, but are still clearly audible to humans as an irritating 'tzeeet'. After a few days the sound becomes wholly ultrasonic, so that the bat's voice breaks to a higher pitch, unlike the human voice which usually gets gruffer with age. Sonar emissions commence at birth in some species, but in others they do not appear for several days; always they precede the ability to fly.

A nursing colony is a bustle of constant noise and movement, bedlam by comparison with the tranquillity of most mammal nurseries. Some species, like *Myotis lucifugus*, can crawl about soon after birth, others may remain quiescent for some days. As soon as they can, the juveniles scurry about exploring the nooks and crannies of their home, increasing their mobility very rapidly as they grow, until at about three weeks they begin their first experimental fluttering flights. They quickly develop the necessary coordination between senses and muscles to perform the complex manoeuvres involved in feeding on the wing. In migratory species, they must also develop the stamina to fly long distances within a few weeks of birth. The young guano bat, for example, must be ready by the autumn to fly hundreds of miles from its birthplace to Mexico for the winter.

Some bats reach maturity in a matter of a few months. Among captive noctules, some females mated at three months and gave birth when a year old (Kleiman and Racey, 1969). In the wild, four out of ten female noctules developed similarly early and gave birth as yearlings (Cranbrook & Barrett, 1965). The rest did not mate until their second year, the normal situation in most temperate-region bats, though some species may not be mature until two years old.

Among all the Microchiroptera, the young vampire is probably the slowest developer. Gestation may last eight months, even though the female does not experience periods of hypothermia brought about by cold weather or food shortage. After birth the young take nine months or more to reach adult size, and even then may not be fully weaned (Schmidt and Manske, 1973). They change from a milk to a blood diet in stages, depending wholly upon milk for the first three months. Later they are fed mouth to mouth with small quantities of blood, and at five or six months old will accompany their mothers and share their meals. Demonstrations of how to feed are not essential; a juvenile born in captivity, and prevented from learning the ghoulish tricks of the vampire trade, still bit a guinea pig and fed from it successfully as soon as the two were introduced.

HOME LIFE IN HUGE COLONIES

Some cave-dwelling species form nursing colonies which number thousands, even millions, of individuals. The most outstanding example is of course the guano bat (*T. brasiliensis*), whose famous and well-studied colony at Carlsbad is in fact relatively small, numbering 'only' 60 to 100,000. Other colonies, notably one at Bracken Cave, Texas (20 million strong in its heyday), rival the largest seabird colonies in size, and as aggregations of terrestrial animals are probably only surpassed by certain social insects.

In such a situation, it is difficult to imagine a specific maternal bond, as seen in other species: how could a female possibly find her own young? Davis (1962) observed that in the enormous nursing colonies of guano bats, returning females would nurse the first babies they found and would not reject approaches made by any of the countless young bats which assailed them from all sides. All the lactating females apparently served as a communal 'dairy herd', providing milk at random. Under such a system the strongest infants would most easily fight off the competition and be fed more often. Perhaps to compensate for this, each female produced up to 16 per cent of her own weight in milk per day, a supply generous enough to enable several babies to be adequately fed and about three times the equivalent performance of the world champion Friesian cow!

A situation where the mothers are indifferent to their own individual offspring, but work indiscriminately for the good of the whole group, is probably without precedent among mammals and is more reminiscent of the totally impersonal socialism exhibited by insects. Although this may be the only feasible way of organising such huge colonies, it does have a pathetic consequence. Any baby which strays from the crèche or falls from the roof will elicit no maternal concern, since none of the females would recognise it as her own and attempt to retrieve it. A helpless, isolated baby guano bat is swiftly engulfed by a multitude of predaceous mites and carnivorous beetles, from whose attentions death must be a welcome relief.

117

The young bats which maintain their hold on the cave walls and ceiling grow rapidly and are ready to fly in about four weeks: they are not taught, and their first attempt is something of a do-or-die proposition. In a large cave, they have about 20–30 metres in which to learn, and they must succeed: once they drop clear of the ceiling they must either fly or fall to the floor below and succumb to the carnivorous multitudes. The task is made even more hazardous by the high aspect-ratio of the guano bat's wing (Chapter 2), poorly suited to manoeuvring or weak flight, though the nursing colonies are usually situated in lofty caves which provide plenty of airspace.

It seems worth wondering why any species forms such large aggregations; and how an investigator makes a census of the multitudes. The first question is at least partially answered by remembering that even in small colonies it is advantageous for the babies to cluster together to conserve heat, and in the big clusters of guano bats the temperature may be several degrees higher than the surrounding air. Perhaps the principal advantage of these vast colonies lies in the communal heat from adults and juveniles helping to accelerate the already rapid growth of the young bats.

As for estimating the population size, one method involves watching the bats as they leave the roost, counting the number in a certain length of the emergent cloud, and timing the speed and total duration of the emergent flight. This is tricky when the bats are coming out at the rate of 5,000 per minute; the calculation requires acceptance of various suppositions and estimations, and anyway it excludes non-volant young that stay behind in the roost. Inside caves better estimates have been made, using a device which projects a known-area patch of light on the roof. Using this, the area covered by bats can be determined and knowing from previous experiments that the dense masses contain about 250 bats per square foot, a simple calculation gives a fair estimate of total population size. A crude index of population size is provided by the amount of guano that accumulates daily on trays placed below the bats.

Although no other bat colonies reach quite the same proportions as those of *T. brasiliensis*, some of the Australian flying foxes gather in great 'camps' during the breeding season. Some of the best known are formed by *Pteropus poliocephalus*, a notable migratory species which moves south into Queensland and New South Wales in the spring. They hang along the branches of well-spaced trees in the open coastal forests. The colonies assemble in traditional sites, often extending for many hundreds of metres, with both sexes present in the breeding groups, some of which may contain upwards of 50,000 individuals (Ratcliffe, 1932). The males are fertile all year round, and on arrival at the camp each sets up a defended territory among the tree branches, marking his particular perches with scent from the shoulder glands. There is intense aggression and threat display within the camp until boundaries are learned and mutual respect established. The females are only fertile from January to March, and take up residence in ones and twos within the territories of individual males, which by this time have been delimited as sections of branch a yard or two long.

The young are born, one per female, after a gestation period of about six months. They cannot fly and despite their weight (up to 400g compared with the 700g mother) are carried, for a week or more, when the female goes off to feed. Later they are left behind, and their cries attract the mothers when they return; each will land, check the identity of the baby bat by smell, and accept or reject it. After about three weeks the young bat becomes non-specific in its attentions and will clamber on any female within reach; but the mothers are still able to recognise their own offspring and often repel 'foreign' young. The juveniles begin to fly around within the camp at about three months old, then accompany the adults on nocturnal feeding flights, becoming progressively more independent, till they are weaned at about four months.

In these pteropodids there is a strong and specific maternal bond, as in many of the Microchiroptera. Despite the confusion of living in great colonies, the bats find and recognise each other individually. This is still possible for the fruit bats, yet not for dense colonies of guano bats, probably because guano bats inhabit dark caves where they could see little (even if their eyesight was good), in a dense two-dimensional mass with no internal divisions or landmarks. The fruit bats have excellent vision and can use it to advantage since their colonies are in the open. They can easily see what they are doing, and so incidentally can the human observer; hence the detail of the behavioural observations possible (Nelson, 1965). Furthermore since the males are present, and they distinguish discrete territorial areas, each family group has a specific home within the camp. Finding this home is made easier by visual recognition at a considerable distance, and also because the colonies are spaced out in three dimensions, not crammed into a single layer, and the trees themselves (unlike a smooth-walled cave) provide many recognisable landmarks.

SOCIAL BEHAVIOUR

Social organisation within these fruit-bat camps is not limited to the level of individual family groups. The whole colony is organised, with separate peripheral groups of immatures and non-breeding adults. On the outskirts of the camp non-territorial males act as 'guards'. They are alert to the slightest disturbance, and, having performed a visual inspection, give a loud alarm signal or remain still, keeping a wary eye open. This complex arrangement of the whole colony's territorial behaviour, and the frequent sniffing at each other's scent glands to establish personal recognition, represent high levels of social organisation, the equal of almost any other non-human society. Even away from the camps, when the bats are in flight they remain together in long processions, whose leaders constantly change yet retain their direction of flight. Whilst watching a small party of epauletted fruit bats (*Epomophorus gambianus*) flying among fig trees in Ethiopia, we noticed how they all showed great concern when one of the

120

group was shot, and gathered round swooping low to inspect it, another sign of group affinity rather than totally independent behaviour.

A higher level of group coordination and behaviour is perhaps expected in fruit bats which live in large aggregations, and feed in relatively localised places where fruit is available. The food of insectivorous bats is widely dispersed and does not require them to operate closely together.

Among the Microchiroptera there is as yet no evidence of complex social organisation, though there are small indications that behaviour in bat colonies is not totally random. For instance, thousands of bats at Carlsbad emerge from the cave in an anti-clockwise spiral and depart in an orderly column, rather than fly out in a disorganised mass.

Homing ability (Chapter 6), the tendency for widely dispersed populations to gather together at certain times of year, and the fidelity which some individuals exhibit toward specific hibernation sites, all suggest some kind of 'loyalty' or attractive behaviour which prevents the animals from behaving as completely independent units. Many Microchiroptera form single-sex groups, the females showing pronounced parental behaviour, but these are not signs of a well-developed social organisation and are usually only seasonal phenomena. Some signs of social behaviour were reported in a group of *Myotis adversus* in Australia which conveniently chose to live in separately recognisable holes in the wall of a railway tunnel (Dwyer, 1970). Each hole contained only one resident adult male at a time. Each individual male had his own favourite hole, and many showed signs of fighting in defence of their home. The breeding females were in groups of up to twelve living with their chosen mate in his hole in the wall, though they were not very faithful wives, often being caught the following month with a different spouse elsewhere in the railway tunnel! This social structure is somewhat akin to that of fur-seal breeding colonies.

Perhaps other bats behave the same way, or maybe there is a

peck order and some genuine, if unsophisticated, social organisation among certain microchiropteran nursing colonies, but many details of bat behaviour remain a mystery. Perhaps with the increasing availability of night-viewing equipment, we will learn more. Already it is possible to use infra-red lamps, whose light is invisible to mammals, to 'floodlight' objects and render them clearly visible through specially sensitised electronic binoculars, or 'passive infra-red' devices which detect and enormously magnify the heat emitted by warm objects.

Better still are the electronic image-intensifiers, like those fitted to television cameras for use in poor light conditions. With these special 'snooperscopes' one can watch bats in flight at 100 metres or more, on the darkest night; or view details of their behaviour in the inky blackness of an old attic. These devices are very costly and are unlikely to be widely used for such frivolous tasks as the study of family life among bats. However, cheap image-intensifiers may become available, and they could provide the key to a whole new range of bat studies, in an area of chiropteran biology which both needs and promises greater advances than any other.

CHAPTER 6

RINGING AND POPULATION STUDIES

How confusing it is to look upon a seething mass of bats; even counting them is difficult, never mind recognising individuals. How tantalising it is to see just one bat hanging in a cave, and not to know if it is the same one that was there last year. How often does it come to this place? How old is it and how much longer might it live? What frustration when all the bats disappear from their hibernaculum, only to reappear the following season! Where have they been meanwhile and what have they been doing? How did they find their way back, or are they a fresh batch that came here by accident?

The investigation of such problems can be rewarding, but requires that each animal be given a clearly recognisable identity. In bats a metal band or 'ring' is attached to the forearm. The usual bat ring is a C-shaped metal clip on which is stamped a serial number and also an address so that members of the public may know where to report if a bat is found. The ring is pinched loosely over the bat's forearm, and its size is chosen so that it does not constrict the propatagium or impede the bat's movements.

Aluminium has been commonly used but the bat is often irritated by the ring and may chew at it vigorously. This can result in the obliteration of the serial number and more important, the production of jagged edges which can cause serious wounding of the flight membranes. This problem is usually most acute among the larger bats which have strong teeth. British bat rings are now made in four sizes from a hard magnesium alloy which forms very smooth and tooth-resistant bands. So far, after extensive field trials, no serious damage either to or resulting from these rings has been reported, although because of the risk of physical damage to the bat, proliferation of ringing projects has been discouraged in Britain, whilst the ringing of birds (whose horny legs are more resistant to ring damage) has progressively increased in recent years. The disturbance associated with bat banding, if not the rings themselves, is a serious imposition on the bats, especially during hibernation (see Chapters 4 & 8), and this must be weighed against the possible benefits derived from bat ringing.

Even with the old-style rings there are plenty of bats flying about today with rings they have carried for fifteen or even twenty years. Large numbers of bats have been ringed in many countries (eg 100,000 guano bats in the United States; over 73,000 little brown bats in New England; 11,000 of twenty-two species in Russia; 7,000 mouse-eared bats in Germany, and so on). In the USA over a quarter of a million rings were issued in 1962 alone. Australia, European and some Iron Curtain countries have their own bat-ringing programmes. Some investigations date back to the mid-1930s, and in Britain the pioneers were John and Win Hooper of the Devon Speleological Society; they have ringed over 3,200 Devon bats since the autumn of 1948.

Once a bat has been banded it carries its own unique identification number. Whenever it is recaptured, wherever it goes and however long it lives, this bat will always be individually recognisable and we can gain a great deal of information about its life history, habits and movements. If enough are marked it becomes possible to study basic aspects of whole populations.

When some bats are ringed, conjecture can be supplemented with proven fact and the study of bat population biology has been largely dependent upon information gained from this method.

MORTALITY FACTORS AND LONGEVITY

Various bizarre deaths have been recorded for bats, including being run over, spiked on cacti and barbed wire, eaten by birds, caught by snakes and frogs, drowned in an attic cistern and trapped in a spider's web. Also of course the gassing and sealing off of colonies results in mass extermination. Many bats must die very young, as a result of desertion or inadequate nutrition by their mothers. Despite these hazards, survival from year to year by the adult bat seems reasonably assured. If there is any one time of particular risk, it must be the end of winter, when fat reserves may be totally depleted, and fickle weather may prevent both continued hibernation and effective feeding. Migratory species are similarly at risk when they reach the end of their long journeys, though they usually take at least some food en route.

How long do bats normally live and how can we tell the age of an individual? By the time they are weaned young bats resemble their parents, although fur colouration may differ for a few months. By the end of summer some of the young are still smaller than adults; more reliably, they still betray signs of immaturity in their bones. When the wing of a young bat is spread in front of a bright light the tips of the finger bones are seen to form caps (epiphyses), which are separated by a small gap from the main shaft of the bone. In older bats—usually within a few months of birth—these detached caps join solidly with the rest of the bone. Among bats with closed epiphyses, sub-adults may sometimes be recognised from the condition of their reproductive organs, but it is impossible to tell the age of fully adult bats. Studies of tooth-wear, eye-lens weights and other criteria of old age have yielded equivocal results with bats, and detailed microscopical examination for growth lines in teeth and bone have so far not been made on a large scale. These techniques are anyway only applicable to dead bats.

Our knowledge of the actual age of individuals comes from ringing studies. For example, one of the earliest bats to be ringed in

Britain was a greater horseshoe (*Rhinolophus ferrumequinum*), first caught in March 1949 and still living in Devon in October 1967 aged at least $19\frac{1}{4}$ years (Hooper & Hooper, 1967). This is not an isolated case of extreme age; enough of this species have now been recaptured after 16 years or more to suggest that the maximum lifespan probably exceeds 20 years. Among British vespertilionids some impressive records have also been established, topped by a Daubentons bat (*Myotis daubentoni*), still alive in 1967 having carried a ring for 18 years. As bat banding has been in progress for much longer in continental Europe and the United States, some of the best longevity records are held by bats in these areas, the oldest one reported so far being an American bat (*Myotis lucifugus*) aged 24 years (Griffin & Hitchcock, 1965).

A common shrew with a body weight of say 8g may live for a year but will die of old age soon after, even when protected from predators; less than 1 per cent of the shrew population last beyond about 14 months. Yet ringing has proved that a small insectivorous bat of similar size may easily live over ten times as long. It has been suggested that hibernation helps delay ageing, because in winter the bat's physiology is 'switched off'; in addition many bats are torpid most of the time even in summer, and are only working in physiological top gear for perhaps four hours each day. Experiments with invertebrates have indeed shown that their average lifespan is increased when they are kept cool and inactive. However, Herreid (1964) compared *Tadarida brasiliensis*, which does not regularly hibernate, with *Myotis lucifugus*, which does. He suggested that the former is a very busy beast, consuming 4,3000,000 calories of energy per year (excluding that spent on migratory flights), about eight times the annual consumption of the latter species; yet there is little or no difference between their potential lifespans. Temperate and tropical bats seem to have similar lifespans and, in captivity at least, many fruit bats reach a ripe old age of 20 years or more, yet they do not hibernate. Longevity of bats may be associated with their low reproductive rate: see Chapter 5.

When enough bats have been ringed, recaptures in successive seasons will demonstrate general trends in the population as a whole, as well as in individuals. For example, juvenile bats are evidently more likely to die, perhaps because they often enter hibernation later than adults and at lower body weights (with less fat reserves). Their survival over the first winter may be poor, perhaps 35 per cent of them dying before their first birthday. Those which survive then stand a good chance of reaching old age: more than 70 per cent of adults may survive from one year to the next. A study of the population dynamics of *Pipistrellus subflavus* by Wayne Davis (1966) provides a nice example, and shows the overall survival/mortality pattern to be rather like that of early human populations before the advent of modern medicine, with high mortality rates among the very young and very old and a good survival rate among the middle-aged (fig 24). This type of study is based upon hibernating animals, but we have already seen (Chapter 4) how behavioural differences between sex and age groups could affect the results. However, few published life-tables for mammals, if any, are free from criticism: sampling bias is almost inevitable, and the true mortality patterns of bats are probably not too dissimilar to those revealed by Davis.

When enough bats have been ringed, the recapture data can be subjected to mathematical analysis to calculate various population statistics. Survival rates, expectation of life in different age groups and sexes, likely maximum life-span, total population size and age of maturity—all these can be predicted. The larger the samples of marked bats, the greater the likely level of accuracy. One of the best examples is the analysis of over 15 years of bat banding in the Netherlands by Bezem, Sluiter & Van Heerdt (1960). From the proportions of marked bats recaptured each year, they were able to calculate life-tables for four species. The adult survival rate for small *Myotis* species was around 75 per cent per year, but less than 60 per cent for lesser horseshoes (*Rhinolophus hipposideros*). It was possible to predict mathematically that about 1 per cent of Daubenton's bats may exceed

20 years of age, whereas in the lesser horseshoe bat mortality was much higher and only 1 per cent was likely to exceed about 8

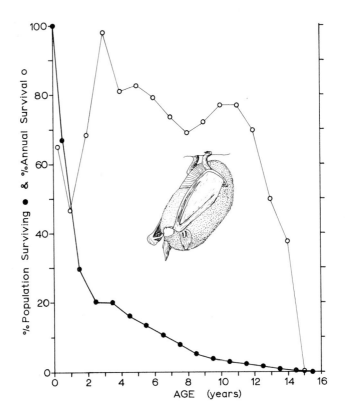

Fig 24. Survival curve for male *Pipistrellus subflavus* (after Davis, W. H. 1966). Survival in the first six months of life is only about 65% and falls to 47% over the first winter. Thereafter the bats stand a 70 to 80% chance of surviving from one year to the next, until about twelve years old.

years. Survival rates were similar in males and females. It should be stressed that this type of information is derived from mathematical treatment of recapture data; the study had not been in progress long enough to get 10 out of 1,000 Daubenton's bats living over 20 years, but with sufficiently large samples showing the proportions of the marked population which survive to 2, 3, 10 years and so on, it was possible to predict the numbers that would live to greater ages.

These calculations stand up to testing from another direction. If we assume a stable population and a constant mortality rate, a female (producing 1 young per year, giving birth for the first time at 1 year old) would have to live just over 2 years to replace herself and her mate (ie through two breeding seasons and the time taken to wean her second baby). If an average female survives 2 years, this would represent an annual survival rate of 75 per cent in the population as a whole; very close to the value calculated for three *Myotis* species. A survival rate of 60 per cent or less, as in the case of the lesser horseshoe, must be balanced by the frequent occurrence of twins or else the population will decline: a decline was in fact observed among the Dutch bats.

A 75 per cent adult survival rate per annum means that about 1 bat in 100 will live to 15 years and 1 per 1,000 would reach 24 years; which as we have already seen is the maximum life-span actually recorded for a bat.

MIGRATION

The existence of long-distance migrations among birds such as swallows, cuckoos, warblers and even tiny humming birds, has been established for some time, largely by ringing studies. The birds apparently follow the good weather southwards and return at the end of winter. Insectivorous bats face similar problems of winter food supplies; they are similar in size to the small migrant birds and some are also strong fliers. Why should they not migrate in the same way? In fact there is circumstantial evidence that a few species do just that. In Russia, flocks of noctules arrive and disappear seasonally with the regularity and prominence that we take for granted in swifts and swallows. Bats are found among flocks of migrant birds attracted to lighthouses at night, and they are often observed at coastal places flying purposefully out to sea where little food and no roosting sites exist. They have been found on board lightships and other vessels many miles from land. The only records of the parti-coloured bat (*Vespertilio murinus*) in Britain this century are from a North Sea oil rig over 150 miles off the north-east coast of England (and nearly 200 miles from the nearest part of the Continent); and an earlier specimen which was found in Shetland. American hoary bats (*Lasiurus cinereus*) have appeared in Iceland and the Orkneys, having presumably flown across from Canada. *Lasiurus* and *Lasionycteris* occasionally visit Bermuda 750 miles off the coast of north Carolina in spring and autumn. Such flights are probably aided by prolonged westerly winds which also bring vagrant American birds to Britain from time to time.

These records prove only that certain bats may travel long distances, not that they undertake true migratory flights which should be regular, markedly seasonal and involve the movement of whole populations out of an area *and back again* sometime later. Long-distance flight records are a clue to migrating behaviour, and circumstantial evidence may strengthen the case for its existence. For instance the hoary bat is found in Alaska and northern Canada in summer, yet from November till April almost all records of this species are from south of latitude 37°N. This suggests that the population must spread northwards hundreds of miles each summer and return south again each winter. (Incidentally, such movements of whole populations can cause confusion when comparing distribution maps of different species or when compiling faunal lists. For example, in Arizona there are 28 species of bats, but only 15 are definitely present all year round.)

To clinch the matter, over the last forty years enough information has accumulated from the recapture of ringed bats to show patterns of migration in considerable detail for certain species, but these mostly concern 'local' migrations among the cave-dwelling bats, where both outward and return journeys have been demonstrated. The concentration of bats in caves during the winter enables large numbers to be ringed fairly easily, and their dispersal in spring is monitored by investigators and the general public locating the marked bats in their summer roosts later in the year.

Perhaps the biggest study of this kind involved banding over 70,000 little brown bats in New England (Davis & Hitchcock, 1965). The results showed that the population which overwinters in the Mount Aeolus cave in Vermont scatters in all directions (though mainly to the south-east, following the contours of the land) in the spring. Although the majority of recaptures were recorded within a 50 mile radius of the cave, some bats were recorded from up to 172 miles away (fig 25). In summer this species likes to live in sun-warmed roofs and closely packed in crevices and behind wooden shuttering. By searching such places at the appropriate time of year, many recoveries of ringed bats were made, and at the same time, more individuals could be banded which later reappeared back at Aeolus cave.

Prime habitats for the little brown bat are those near woodland and water where insect food abounds, yet the winter is usually spent in caverns. From the ringing studies it is clear that the Mount Aeolus cave habitués are drawn in from a very large catchment area; 75 per cent of the recaptures were made within an area of 8,600 square miles, the remaining 25 per cent even further afield. In areas where caves are scarce, a single one may harbour large populations of bats (300,000 in the case of the Aeolus cave), drawn in from great distances: in Denmark, for instance, the Daubjerg limestone mines attract bats from summer colonies over 50 miles away. Ringing studies thus reveal just how vital are the protection and conservation of good hibernation sites to the bats of a very wide area.

Seasonal migratory patterns in a north-south direction have been nicely demonstrated in *Myotis sodalis*, where large numbers banded in the caves of Kentucky have been recaptured up to 350 miles away at various summer colonies, all of them almost due

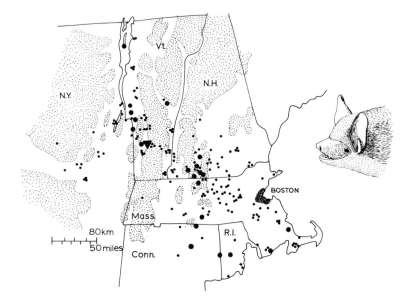

Fig 25. The dispersal of little brown bats (*Myotis lucifugus*) banded in the hibernaculum on Mt Aeolus (triangle). Small spots indicate single recoveries, larger spots represent the recovery of four or more individuals. (After Davis & Hitchcock, 1965.) Shaded areas indicate land over 1,000 feet high, which the bats apparently tend to avoid.

north in Indiana, Ohio and Michigan. A few bats were ringed in the caves, recaptured in the summer colonies, then caught once more back in the hibernaculum where they were first found, thus demonstrating conclusively a true 'round trip' migratory cycle.

Strictly cavernicolous bats such as the greater horseshoe (*Rhinolophus ferrumequinum*) are so dependent upon specific hibernacula that their distribution, in Britain especially, is limited by the availability of caves and is closely tied to the distribution of the limestone rocks in which they occur. Ringing recoveries show that despite its large size this species rarely travels any distance; most remain within 20 miles of where they were first caught. The Hoopers' studies (1956) of ringed horseshoe bats in Devon, England, again show seasonal migrations between favourite haunts, but only short distances are involved (fig 26). Recoveries have shown that individual bats may make a 'tour' of various caves and mines during a single winter, spending a little time hibernating in each.

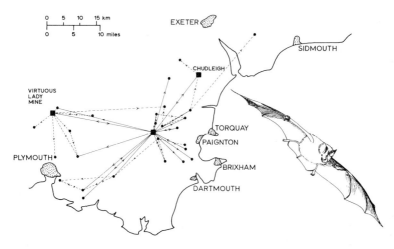

Fig 26. Recoveries of banded greater horseshoe bats (*Rhinolophus ferrumequinum*) in Devon, England. Many bats were ringed around Buckfastleigh (central square) and recorded movements of individuals from there are shown in solid lines. Double arrows indicate that the same bat also returned to Buckfastleigh; dashed lines show flights between additional study sites, revealing a complex pattern of movements. (After Hooper & Hooper, 1956.)

Gregarious cave-dwelling bats are an easy subject for large-scale investigations, but there have also been some successes with non-cavernicolous species like the tree-dwelling noctule (*Nyctalus noctula*), in which the same bats have been caught at both ends of their journeys between summer and winter quarters, some 40 miles apart. Local migrations may take place during the summer, especially if a colony is disturbed. Sluiter & Van Heerdt (1966) found that noctules were continually changing their tree roosts even when undisturbed. This went on, surprisingly, well into the period when females were pregnant and even when they were nursing their young; the babies were transported distances of several miles when their mothers changed roosts. In winter the noctules could survive in clusters inside hollow trees and woodpecker holes, even when the temperature outside fell to −14°C, so seasonal migration to warmer areas was not essential and most of the bats in fact stayed put. However, there were several long-distance recoveries of ringed noctules, one juvenile female being recaptured 562 miles (900km) south-south-west. So at least some of the bats undertook long-distance flights, even though they could apparently have survived back home.

These recoveries do not indicate a consistent long-distance movement by either juveniles or adults, nor is one sex more likely to move than the other. For species like the noctule which live in trees and houses, there should be no shortage of roosting sites and certainly no need to go great distances. Sluiter & Van Heerdt suggested that their bats might have flown away because of disturbance caused by their own ringing work, but if so the one that went 562 miles from Utrecht to Bordeaux must have been very scared indeed! The explanation may have something to do with population dispersal. The noctule is one of the few temperate-zone bats that regularly produce twins. Perhaps twins represent 'over-production': long-distance emigration flights might be a way of avoiding excessive population densities in the home area. Or, simpler still, some bats may just get lost and fly long distances in the wrong direction, making a one-way trip, not a true migration.

Many bat species that live alone or in small groups prefer to hibernate in hollow trees or old buildings. Such hibernacula are usually fairly abundant and widely distributed. Gregarious species, especially those which spend the winter underground in the humid warmth of caves, may have to travel some way. Yet in summer it may be advantageous for the population to disperse as widely as possible to avoid excessive competition for food in the immediate vicinity of the winter quarters. A seasonal pattern thus emerges: grouping in winter, scattering in summer. Similar seasonal aggregations and dispersal are seen in the formation each year of nursing colonies (where the young are born in traditional locations) and their disbanding once the young are weaned. But many species do not follow a clear-cut pattern, and not all members of the same population behave the same way.

Inconsistent behaviour may cause us to wonder again about the underlying purpose of migratory flights. Banding studies of the immense populations of the guano bat in the southern United States have proved conclusively that they move southwards in the autumn after their young are weaned, flying purposefully up to 500 miles in less than a fortnight. In spring they return from Mexico to the great nursing colonies of the USA. Although most of the bats, millions of them, undertake these journeys, many thousands do not, remaining in the caves of Texas and Arizona to hibernate. Thousands of others fail to make the northerly migration and stay to breed in Mexico. Why do they stay behind? Is it the same ones that do so every year? If they can do it, why not others too and how is it 'decided' how many shall not migrate?

In addition to throwing light on the existence and nature of true migratory movements among populations, recaptures of individual ringed bats provide the opportunity to measure total straight-line distances flown; certain species are revealed as regular long-distance fliers, whilst other are more static. Among the small European *Myotis*, which are very similar to each other in size and appearance, recaptures reveal interesting differences in wanderlust. In the Netherlands, *Myotis mystacinus* has been recovered up to 20 miles away from the South Limburg limestone mines and *M. emarginatus* a similarly modest distance, 55 miles. *Myotis daubentoni* has done rather better, 97 miles; but *M. dasycneme*, sharing the same mines in winter, were energetic travellers, appearing in places over 200 miles away to the SSW, and at many different sites in a variety of other directions (56 miles SW; 84 miles NW; 136 miles NNW; 122 miles SE).

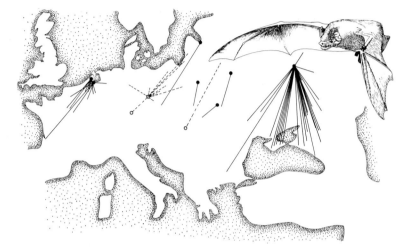

Fig 27.   Recorded long-distance movements of noctules (*Nyctalus noctula*) in Europe. Bats banded at summer roosts (solid circles) tend to move S or SW in autumn, bats banded in winter roosts (hollow circles) later fly N or NE. (After Strelkov, 1969.)

In Europe the noctule has been shown to make long-distance flights (up to 1,000 miles) comparable to the travels of the similarly large fast-flying *Lasiurus* of North America. In his review of migrations in Russian bats, Strelkov (1969) recorded 27 cases of noctules travelling over 300 miles (fig 27); astonishingly, similar feats were also performed by tiny pipistrelles (*Pipistrellus pipistrellus* & *P. nathusii*). One flew from the Voronezh Reserve in Russia down to Istanbul for the winter, another flew 1,000 miles to Greece! Pipistrelles flying from Russia to Bulgaria also covered large distances (690+miles). The severity of mid-continental winters may necessitate such long migrations. Certainly the harsh climate of eastern Europe forces species like noctules and pipistrelles to seek the shelter of caves during the winter, which they rarely do in Britain.

The fruit bats offer one of the most obvious areas for future work based on ringing studies. All the examples and massive investigations described above refer to microchiropteran species; practically nothing has been done with banded populations of megachiropterans. Fruit bats are tropical animals but some species live in areas with only a limited fruiting season, as in East Africa where the epauletted bat (*Epomophorus*) might feed on figs during the rainy season but in the semi-arid conditions of the rest of the year may have to fly several hundred miles to find a different climate where other trees are still in fruit. The larger pteropodids are certainly strong fliers and *Cynopterus* is known to travel over 70 miles to and from its feeding area in a single night; potentially the megachiroptera are even greater travellers than many of the small bats we have considered so far.

HOMING

The ability to find their way to and from distant places is implicit in the migratory flights of bats, but one may draw the distinction between bats which return, either once or regularly, to the same place of their own accord (eg those migrating between traditional winter and summer roosts), and those which are deliberately displaced by experimenters in order to discover whether (and perhaps how) they can return to where they were first captured.

Certainly bats can find their way home from considerable distances (R. Davis 1966), even some species which do not normally engage in long flights. The longest record for homing seems to be held by the big brown bat (*Eptesicus fuscus*), three of which found their way home after being released 450 miles away. Even the tiny *Myotis lucifugus* can apparently get back home after being displaced up to 270 miles. Indeed, people wishing to get rid of bats from their roofs, and reluctant to kill them, have caught them for release elsewhere, only to find to their dismay that many of them have returned by the following night!

Homing experiments generally demonstrate that the further

137

away bats are released, the fewer of them will return; as in an experiment with *M. sodalis*, where 44 per cent had returned from 12 miles after a few nights, but only 1 per cent from 132 miles. Some may succeed in getting back, but do not return to exactly the same spot, so escaping detection by the investigator. Others show a remarkable tenacity for an exact spot. In our own small bat-ringing study we have seen the same individual bats return annually to the same mine chamber, perhaps even the same crack in the wall. One of our Daubenton's bats has been recaptured in seven different winters; on six of those occasions it was in the same small part of the same mine, even though several other similar places and almost identical galleries were available only a few yards away.

Displacement of ringed bats, like the release of racing pigeons, enables an investigator to measure the time taken to return over a known distance. Some of these experiments have demonstrated *average* flying speeds of almost 20mph, nearly the normal flight speed of the bat, indicating that it must have flown back in almost a straight line without hesitation. In experiments with big brown bats, several returned from 250 miles in four or five nights and in another experiment with *Myotis velifer*, a couple flew 28 miles home in four hours. The European parti-coloured bat (*Vespertilio murinus*) has clocked up 225 miles in two days. Multiple homing flights have also been demonstrated. One female pallid bat (*Antrozous pallidus*) returned from eight different locations, up to 68 miles from home, no doubt thoroughly fed up with the attentions of enthusiastic bat investigators!

How do the bats navigate? Two explanations seem possible:

1. That they know the geography of a considerable area sufficiently well to recognise landmarks and use them to find their way back.

2. That they possess some kind of direction-finding sense which, no matter where it is taken, tells them in which direction home lies—just as a compass needle always 'knows' where the North Pole is.

The second suggestion is an attractive one, considering the

speed with which some homing bats select the correct direction and follow it, but the bats' home emits no useful clue which could identify its location at a distance, so perhaps the bat has an inertial guidance system like that used in submarines. This records the speed, direction and duration of all movements, using a computer, clocks and a stabilised gyro compass. The three-dimensional memory of a journey is thus retained and at any time, by complex computing, the relative positions of ship and base can be quickly determined. If a bat used such a system it would have to remember and analyse all movements made whilst being carried away by the investigator; surely an impossible task in a bag full of squeaking, wriggling bats, with no sight of the outside world and transportation at unfamiliar speeds in a motor car.

Yet is the first suggestion any more likely? A bat taken 250 miles from home can find its way back, but how can it possibly be familiar with the landmarks along that journey? It does not know where it will be released; it could be 250 miles in any direction, so it would have to know the geography of a circle totalling more than 195,000 square miles!

And how could the bat recognise landmarks? Echolocation may resolve fine details of nearby objects (Chapter 7), but echoes from distant things would be very faint. Even supposing that echolocation of objects up to 100 metres away were possible, using high-energy sound emissions, the bat would still have to fly along in a narrow 'corridor' only 200 metres wide, using every tree and building as signposts. The bats must have some means of appreciating the whole scene and their position within it. They must know where the horizon is and the location of major landmarks such as rivers, forests and faraway hills, and may get some general guidance from the moon and stars and the general brightness of certain parts of the sky. It seems likely that some form of learning is involved and homing is not entirely instinctive, since experiments have shown that juveniles are less successful at homing than the adults.

Our appreciation of the environment is mainly through sight, but some of the earliest experiments ever performed on bats, nearly 200 years ago, revealed that blinded bats could still find their way home. Modern experiments confirm blindfolded bats can home from 40 miles or so, but that the number who do so, and their speed, are considerably reduced. (Blindfolding in these experiments is usually accomplished by temporarily painting an opaque substance over the eyes.) Really long-distance homing, 100 miles or more, seems to be impossible with impaired vision. Nevertheless the bats at Carlsbad caverns, returning at dawn, have been observed to plunge directly into ground fog so thick that it completely obscured the cave entrance, suggesting they were not totally reliant on sight.

Many bats frequent very complex caves and mines, where they fly in total darkness and vision is therefore impossible. Some of the mines are built with geometric precision; all corners at right angles, all galleries the same shape. Such labyrinths can be impossibly confusing, as anyone who has had the nasty experience of being lost in one will know. Although echolocation will enable bats to fly without bumping into the walls, in order to find their way out of such an underground maze they must also have some sort of spatial memory; which brings us back to the earlier analogy with submarines, already dismissed as improbable.

Another problem is how bats find and recognise a cave entrance, especially when it is small and overgrown (or the tiny crack that permits access to a house roof or hollow tree). It is unusual to see a bat exploring for such openings, yet when blocked mine tunnels are reopened, the bats may find and occupy them within a few weeks.

Bat ringing has its limitations and we are unlikely to discover anything entirely new without the aid of novel techniques. One promising line of research involves attaching miniature radio transmitters to bats, which then emit a radio signal everywhere they go, from which their position and activity can be monitored continuously without further disturbance to themselves. The method has already yielded much information on the home range and activity patterns of many other mammals. Indeed some animals are now tracked automatically, the data being fed into a computer which prints out home-range maps. This technique would overcome the major disadvantage of bat ringing, that little or nothing is known of the bat's movements between recaptures. It could throw much light on homing and direction-finding abilities, and on flight speed and feeding behaviour. Unfortunately small transmitters with the necessary range of several miles, and able to last for at least a few days, are not yet available at reasonable cost. However, big strong bats (*Phyllostomus hastatus*) have carried transmitters in Trinidad, and been shown to fly straight home over short distances (6 to 10 miles), using visual cues. Over greater distances the bats were less certain of their actions, and blindfolds seriously impaired their navigation. Acoustical orientation evidently enabled the bats to return home, over moderate distances at least, but vision was the main navigational sense. The same study was used to investigate feeding journeys (Williams & Williams, 1970). Radio tracking would be an excellent way to find out more about the Megachiroptera, mostly strong fliers and big enough to carry a small (say 5g) transmitter. Since they are known to rely on eyesight rather than hearing, their habits and homing abilities would make an interesting comparison with those of the microchiropterans so intensively studied hitherto.

CHAPTER 7

SEEING WITH SOUND

That bats find their way in the dark and hunt insects by echolocation is now general knowledge. But the proper investigation and
understanding of this behaviour has only been possible since the
development of electronic equipment needed for radio and radar.

It is surprising, and salutary, to find that as long ago as 1794 the
Italian Spallanzani, together with several of his correspondents,
had demonstrated convincingly that bats must use some such
non-visual navigation system. Spallanzani had observed that
while owls were incapable of flying in complete darkness, bats
could do so perfectly well; in 1793 he captured a number of bats
in a local roost, blinded them, and released them in the same
place. Four days later he revisited the roost in the early morning
and captured a number of his blinded animals. When he dis-
sected them he found that their stomachs were just as full as those
of the intact bats which he also found. Obviously, the bats did not
need their sight to hunt successfully. Spallanzani circulated his
observations, and the most important reaction came from
Geneva, where the surgeon Jurine reported that he had successfully repeated Spallanzani's experiments with blinded bats, but
added that when he blocked the bats' ears with wax, they blun-
dered into objects quite helplessly. Spallanzani repeated Jurine's

experiment and was surprised to confirm his results. Moreover, he found that when the ear plugs were removed the bats recovered their ability to fly without bumping into things. He then devised perhaps the most remarkable experiment of all: he plugged the ears of the bats with small brass tubes. The bats were still able to navigate successfully, indicating that the discomfort did not seriously upset them, but when Spallanzani blocked the tubes they were once more rendered helpless. He was at a loss to explain these results; bats were silent in flight, so why should they need their ears?

Other biologists were sceptical and the influential Cuvier, in 1800, dismissed the clear results which Spallanzani and Jurine had so painstakingly obtained (without carrying out any experiments of his own), by supposing that the sense of touch explained the bat's ability to avoid obstacles. Spallanzani had in fact already tried to implicate the sense of touch, but he found, for instance, that coating the wings with varnish or flour paste had little effect on flight. Yet it was Cuvier's opinion that was accepted for the next 120 years, and while Spallanzani's observation that blinded bats flew satisfactorily was respected, the equally important point that deaf ones couldn't was forgotten.

What was missing, of course, was the realisation that there could be sounds which were inaudible to the human ear, yet detectable by bats. The English physiologist Hartridge was intrigued one night when a bat flew into his room at Cambridge. He knew of sonar (asdic) which had been developed during World War I to detect submarines, and he made the suggestion that bats might use high-frequency sounds of short wavelength to detect insects and obstacles by their echoes, but it was a further eighteen years before he was proved right. Detection of these sounds required first the development of a suitable microphone and the means of rendering them audible to humans. Donald Griffin, an undergraduate at Harvard in 1938, was interested in bat-banding work and the problems of bat navigation. It happened that in the Harvard Physics Department a pioneer of the study of 'supersonic' sounds, Professor G. W. Pierce, had developed what was then perhaps the only apparatus suitable for detecting such emissions and was himself working on insect sounds. (It has since been agreed by physicists that 'supersonic' shall be used to describe *speeds* in excess of sound in air, and 'ultrasonic' to describe *sounds*.) Griffin and Pierce put bats in front of the apparatus, and found that bats indeed produced ultrasonic sounds; but they suggested, over-cautiously, that the bats might be using them for communication (Pierce and Griffin, 1938). This marked the start of a large (and continuing) body of research work, much of it carried out by Griffin, his colleagues and students, and described by Griffin himself in his excellent book *Listening in the Dark* (1958), upon which this chapter relies heavily.

By one of those odd quirks of coincidence which occur quite often in science, almost the same discovery was made by a Dutch zoologist, Dijkgraaf. He did not have the benefit of Pierce's detector for ultrasonic sound, nor since Holland was under wartime occupation at the time was he aware of the work going on at Harvard. However, he did know of Spallanzani's experiments and himself repeated the one of blocking the ears. It happens that the ultrasonic sounds which bats produce do in fact include a small component audible to humans, rather similar to the ticking of a wrist watch. Dijkgraaf not only heard this faint sound being emitted by bats in flight, but noticed an increased rate of ticking when the bats were carrying out some difficult manoeuvre. As a result he suggested that these faint sounds were used by bats for echolocation, and it was only when international scientific communications were restored after the war that the relationship of these faint ticks to the ultrasonic sounds was established.

The story contains one other coincidence. The development of human airborne echolocation (called radar or RDF) by Sir Robert Watson-Watt and his colleagues was just about contemporaneous with the experiments on bats. Initial attempts to detect aircraft were carried out in 1935 and the early radar stations were set up around south-east England in 1936 and 1937.

THE PHYSICS OF ECHOLOCATION

Biologists are usually not very good at physics; but it is impossible to talk about the echolocation behaviour of bats without some understanding of the physics of sound.

Frequency

Sound is made up of disturbances or vibrations in the medium through which it is passing. The molecules of the medium are alternately compressed and expanded—imagine the prongs of a tuning fork vibrating back and forth, impressing their movements on the air around them. If one were to measure either the air pressure as the sound waves pass, or the density of the air molecules, the resultant graph would show regular peaks and troughs, in other words cycles of high and low pressure or density. The pitch or frequency of a sound depends on the number of such cycles per second. A low sound has fewer: for example 'middle C' on the piano has a frequency of 256 cycles per second, while the C one octave higher has a frequency of 512 cycles per second. In fact 'cycles per second' are now called Herz (Hz), the same thing but a shorter name. Human hearing extends over a range from about 20Hz to 20,000Hz. The frequencies which bats use are mostly in the inaudible (ultrasonic) range above 20,000Hz, abbreviated further to 20 kiloherz (kHz, ie 1,000 Herz, equal to the more familiar 'kilocycles per second'). The normal frequencies used by bats range between 20kHz and 130kHz, with extremes of 12kHz and 160kHz.

Wavelength

Another way of specifying the pitch of a sound is to measure the distance between successive peaks of high pressure. This measurement, in metres or millimetres, is termed the wavelength. A high-frequency sound has very short wavelengths, while a low-frequency sound has long wavelengths. This use of two different measures for basically the same property of the sound is familiar—many radios are marked in 'metres' (ie wavelength) on the long and medium wavebands but in kHz (ie frequency) on the 'shortwave' scale.

Sound travels in air at roughly 344 metres per second (c760 miles per hour) and the speed of sound (V) is the product of the frequency (F) and wavelength (λ): $V = F\lambda$. This emphasises the fact that wavelength and frequency are inversely related to one another, and moreover that the relationship is a linear one.

Harmonics

So far, we have talked about sounds composed of only one frequency or wavelength at a time. In practice life is much more complicated; for a start, a bat can vary the frequency of the sound it produces just as, for example, we can sing high and low notes. In addition, the production of a pure sound in nature is actually quite difficult—an object vibrated at say 200Hz tends to vibrate also, 'in sympathy', at 400Hz, 600Hz and so on, that is at frequencies twice, three times, etc, the base frequency. In such a series the base frequency is referred to as the fundamental and the others as the second, third, etc, harmonics. The richness of sound from an organ pipe, for example, is due to the many harmonics which accompany the fundamental. Harmonics accompany our own speech and most bat echolocation sounds; but some bats seem to be able to suppress either the fundamental or its harmonics almost completely, and so produce a pure note.

Amplitude

One other property of sound is the energy it contains: its loudness or amplitude. Just as we can whistle quietly or loudly on the same note, so bats can produce 'quiet' or 'loud' ultrasonic pulses. Since they are silent to us, we have to measure their loudness with some form of instrument. In terms of the sound-wave model, we measure the difference in pressure between the wave's peak and trough. The usual unit of pressure used to be 'dynes per square centimetre'. Nowadays 'Newtons per square metre' (1 Newton = 10^5 dynes) is a more correct term. Another measure of sound intensity is the 'decibel', but this is not an absolute scientific unit, like a dyne; instead it is a comparison of two levels of sound as heard by a microphone. A decibel is defined as 20 times the log of the ratio of the two sound pressures being compared, and the usual base for comparison is the faintest sound which can just be heard by the human ear (this has a pressure of 0.0002 dynes per square centimetre).

Examining Ultrasonic Sounds

Since the sounds a bat produces are for the most part inaudible to humans, one needs some special receiver like Pierce's even to realise that the bat is emitting them. A simple bat detector can be made by adapting an ordinary transistor radio, with the addition of a suitably sensitive microphone. When tuned to an appropriate frequency the radio produces an audible click in response to each ultrasonic chirp from a bat. Further analysis of such a chirp requires either an oscillograph or a sound spectrograph. The oscillograph record shows the pressure changes during each pulse as a series of waves, while the spectrograph plots the frequencies used against time, and also indicates amplitude by the blackness of the trace.

ECHOLOCATION IN VESPERTILIONID BATS

With so much work now being done on echolocation in bats and in other mammals (Busnel, 1967), it is becoming increasingly difficult to keep abreast of the latest developments. One approach is to describe the pattern of echolocation behaviour shown by such well-studied vespertilionid species as the little brown bat (*Myotis lucifugus*) and big brown bat (*Eptesicus fuscus*). This will provide a base with which the different behaviour of other bats can be compared.

Eptesicus fuscus generally hunts back and forth along a fairly regular beat, perhaps 30 metres above the ground. Listening through the bat detector to such a bat in cruising flight, one hears a steady 'tut tut tut' as short pulses of ultrasonic sound are emitted. These pulses are produced at a fairly slow rate, perhaps four or five per second, but every so often the bat dives or twists away from its regular beat; it is a strong presumption that it is chasing an insect. Over the bat detector the previously steady 'tut tut tut' accelerates rapidly, ending in a sharp buzz. More scientifically, the pulse repetition rate increases from 4–5/sec to as many as 200/sec. Griffin has divided up such sequences arbitrarily into the search phase (the steady period with a low pulse-repetition rate), the intermediate approach phase and the terminal phase (the buzz or 'raspberry'), shown in fig 28.

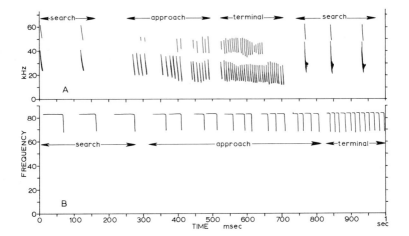

Fig 28.   Sonargrams showing the search, approach and terminal phases of a hunt in *Eptesicus fuscus* (A) and *Rhinolophus ferrumequinum* (B). Both bats squeeze in more pulses in the terminal phase. *Eptesicus* does this partly by shortening the amount of frequency drop, but its short pulses can easily be repeated rapidly; it also uses rather lower frequencies in the terminal phase. *Rhinolophus* has such long pulses that these have to be shortened in order to fit them in—it is the constant-frequency part of the pulse which is curtailed most in the terminal phase. (Based on Griffin, 1958 and Schnitzler, 1967.)

Analysis using a spectrograph shows that the bat does not emit sounds of a constant frequency (fig 28). Instead each pulse starts at a frequency of perhaps 60kHz and drops down, through nearly an octave, to 34kHz. The record also shows that this drop in fre-

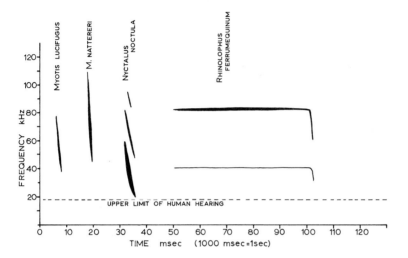

Fig 29. Sonargrams of single echolocation pulses (from the search phase) of four bats. The vespertilionids *Myotis lucifugus, M. nattereri* and *Nyctatus noctula* are frequency modulating (FM) bats—their pulses are extremely short, lasting less than 5msec, yet drop in frequency by 40kHz or more during their emission. By contrast, the pulses of *Rhinolophus* are about ten times as long (50msec) and mostly emitted on a constant frequency, though there is a short frequency drop at the end. Both *Nyctalus* and *Rhinolophus* show harmonic components. Note that all these bats are operating at ultrasonic levels, ie above the upper limit of human hearing.
(After Schnitzler, Pye and others.)

quency occurs in a very short period of time, about 0.01 seconds (10 milliseconds) during the search phase. If there are only four or five pulses per second, and the pulses are each as short as this, then the silent intervals between pulses must be fairly long, about 0.2 seconds (200 milliseconds), hence the slow, steady 'tut tut tut' of the search phase. During the approach and terminal phases, three correlated changes occur: the length of each pulse shortens, to about 1msec, the pulse interval drops to about 5msec (together giving the pulse repetition rate of 200/sec) and the range of the frequency drop during the pulse is reduced to about 5kHz (from 25kHz down to 20kHz). Since the range of human hearing extends up to between 15 and 20kHz, these cries are at the lower limit of the ultrasonic range and are audible to some people.

This pattern of changes makes good sense in terms of echolocation. After each pulse has been emitted, the bat has to wait for any usable echoes before emitting the next pulse. During the search phase, with the bat cruising along a steady course, an occasional pulse with a long listening period seems a sensible procedure. As the bat closes in on its prey, however, it is obviously more important for it to be kept appraised of exactly where it is relative to its prey. The obvious way of doing this is to send out pulses as often as possible. Since it is close to its prey the echoes will return very quickly and short pulses, necessarily crossing a more brief span of frequencies, are needed to enable this rapid accession of information. If we recall that sound in air travels at approximately 340 metres per second, which is 340mm/msec, a search-phase pulse 2msec long occupies a 700mm (28in) long airspace, while the restricted 0.5msec pulse of the terminal phase is only 175mm (7in) long in the air.

To put these data another way, and one perhaps more evidently important to the bat: if the bat is flying at 15m/sec, then in the silent interval of 200 milliseconds between pulses in the search phase, it travels 3 metres (ie 3,000mm or about 10 feet). On the other hand, during the abbreviated 5 millisecond interval in the terminal phase, it would fly only 75mm (3in), giving an insect much less chance of escaping (Table 8).

During the earlier years of the study of bat echolocation, it quickly became clear that the procedure outlined above was being followed by bats dodging obstacles, but some doubt remained as to whether insects were also hunted in this way. The sceptics suggested that the bats were in fact listening to the sound produced by the wing-beat of the insects. Further experiments, particularly with *Myotis lucifugus* catching insects within a flight room (Griffin, Webster & Michael, 1960), have shown the same in-

TABLE 8

Comparison of the echolocation behaviour of *Eptesicus fuscus* during the search and terminal phases (the approach phase is intermediate)

	Search	*Terminal*
Pulse repetition rate	4 or 5 per sec	200 per sec
Pulse length	10m sec	1m sec
Silent interval between pulses	200m sec	5m sec
Frequency sweep within pulse	60–34kHz	25–20kHz
Distance travelled by bat		
(at 15m/sec) between pulses	3,000mm	75mm

crease in pulse-repetition rate, shortening of the pulse, and reduction of the sweep of frequency. These bats were synchronously recorded on ciné-film and in sound, and there is no doubt that they were catching an insect each time a terminal-phase 'buzz' was recorded. If the bats were listening to the sounds produced by the insects they would surely not have indulged themselves in a flourish of sound production. It is still possible that bats do sometimes locate the sounds that the insects themselves produce, but for the most part they do their own searching.

ECHOLOCATION IN OTHER BATS

Rhinolophidae
Most small vespertilionid bats, and also the Molossidae, seem to use approximately the same echolocation procedures as described for *Eptesicus*. In particular they all use pulses which change rapidly in frequency as they are emitted, and they are consequently referred to as frequency-modulating, or FM, bats. Other groups of bats use rather different procedures and in some respects the most complete antithesis to the FM bats is provided by the horseshoe bats (Rhinolophidae).

Like the FM bats, rhinolophids show a change of echolocation behaviour on approaching an obstacle or prey, and one can recognise search, approach and terminal phases (Schnitzler, 1967). During the search phase, the pulses are emitted at about 10 per second, more often than in FM bats, and surprisingly each is very much longer, taking about 50msec to emit. The silent intervals between pulses are thus much shorter than in FM bats, about 50msec, and equal to the pulse in length. While FM bats are silent for 90 per cent of the time during the search phase, horseshoe bats are only silent for 50 per cent of the time, and it is evident that they do not stop emitting to listen for echoes. The pulses themselves differ too; instead of dropping in frequency through an octave, the pulses of horseshoe bats are emitted on a constant frequency for most of the pulse; there is just a short 5msec end to the pulse in which the frequency drops through 29kHz (fig 29). The precise frequency of the constant part of the pulse is a species-specific character. Thus *Rhinolophus ferrumequinum* emits at 83kHz, while *R. hipposideros* uses 119kHz.

During the terminal phase, the rate of pulse emission rises to about 75 pulses/sec, and the duration of each individual pulse drops to about 10msec. The intervals are therefore very short, only about 3msec each. The frequency of the initial part of the pulse does not change, but in shortening of the pulse it is this constant-frequency part which is most curtailed, and the brief frequency-modulated part is accentuated by being emitted more loudly.

There is one other important difference between the FM and the horseshoe bats. Sealing the mouths of FM bats is as effective a means of disorientating them as blocking the ears. This is because the echolocation sounds are produced in the larynx and emitted through the open mouth. It has long been known from anatomical studies that in horseshoe bats the larynx projects internally into the back of the nasal passages. Sealing the mouths of horseshoe bats does not upset their echolocation, while sealing their noses suffocates them! They do, in fact, emit their echolocation pulses through the nostrils and these are positioned half a wavelength apart. In fact, the 'horseshoe' which gives these bats their name, a flap of skin around the nostrils, seems to have the structure and function of a megaphone, causing the sound to be emitted as a concentrated beam.

Megadermatidae

One of the Old World 'false vampire' bats (*Megaderma lyra*) uses a third system (Möhres, 1967). Pulses are very brief: in the search phase about 1.7msec, and in the terminal phase only 0.4msec long. The pulse-repetition rate is irregular: short bursts of pulses being interspersed with long, but variable, silent intervals. Within each burst of pulses, the repetition rate is high, as might be expected with such short pulses, but also very variable. In the search phase, it seems usually to be in the range 30 to 50 per second, but can be as low as 13 per second. In the terminal phase, rates of 90 pulses per second were often recorded and even as high as 300 or more. Within these pulses, the frequency is modulated, so in this respect *Megaderma* resembles the Vespertilionidae. On the other hand, instead of operating at a single frequency, the pulses include two or three frequencies which are related harmonics.

Megaderma resembles *Rhinolophus* in that the echolocation pulses are emitted through the nose and beamed by a (less complicated) noseleaf. It has, however, one further major point of difference from both *Rhinolophus* and the Vespertilionidae. This concerns the loudness of the sounds, that is the amount of energy the bat puts into its 'shouting' (or 'snorting', as it uses its nose). It is not easy to obtain meaningful estimates of the loudness of a bat's noises. Holding a bat in front of a microphone does not necessarily represent its normal performance in flight. For a measurement under natural conditions, the bat has to be flying directly at the microphone and at a known distance from it (since sound intensity falls off with the square of the distance, this is important).

Accepting that the figures may not be directly comparable,

Myotis lucifugus has been recorded at 5–10cm from the microphone producing sounds of about 109 decibels. This is of course, a very loud noise indeed; these bats really do 'shout'. By contrast, only 80 decibels were recorded at distances of 6–15cm from the head of *Megaderma lyra* (Möhres, 1967); the term 'whispering bat' is sometimes used for such 'quiet' species. (Before you object that 80 decibels is the noise level recorded from jet aircraft, bear in mind the fact that you do not usually listen to them at a range of 10cm!) These whispering bats share the habit of feeding on sedentary prey, picking insects off foliage (*Plecotus*) or lizards and rodents off the ground (*Megaderma, Phyllostomus*). It seems possible that they use 'quiet' pulses to avoid swamping the echo from their prey with echoes from the background, but it has also been suggested that if they used 'louder' pulses, they might warn their prey of their approach.

Other systems

Finally, a very different sort of echolocation is practised by the African and Asian fruit bats of the genus *Rousettus*. All the fruit bats (Pteropodidae) have big eyes and obviously use their eyesight for navigation. Most tend to roost in trees and *Rousettus* too has good eyes and uses them whenever possible, but unlike the other pteropodids it roosts in the depths of caves where there is no light at all, and here it uses echolocation. Its sound pulses differ markedly from those of the Microchiroptera, being of low frequency and produced not by the larynx but by the tongue. The pulse is short (up to 5msec) but has no particular structure, no frequency modulation for example, and is a mixture of frequencies from 6.5kHz to 100kHz, most of the energy being in the range 12–18kHz. We hear it as quite a loud 'click', clearly audible several metres away.

Two genera of birds which habitually live and nest in caves, have also developed a system of echolocation using clicks which are audible to humans. These are the South American oil bird (*Steatornis caripensis*) and the swiftlets of south-east Asia (some of the species of *Collocalia*).

TABLE 9

Echolocation in the different groups of bat. A comparison of salient features (based on Novick 1963, etc).

	Frequency type	Pure (P) or Harmonic (H)	Pulse length	Emitted through	Intensity	Food
Rousettus	Audible	Mixed	Short	Mouth	Loud	Fruit
Emballonuridae	Slight FM	H	Short	Mouth	Loud?	Insects
Nycteridae	FM	H	vShort	Nose	Quiet	Insects
Megadermatidae	FM	H	vShort	Nose	Quiet	Insects Small verts.
Hipposideridae	CF or mixed	P²	Long	Nose	Loud	Insects
Rhinolophidae	CF	P²	Long	Nose	Loud	Insects
Natalidae	FM	H	Short	Mouth	Loud?	Insects
Chilonycterinae	FM or CF	H	Long or Short	Mouth	Loud	Insects
Phyllostominae	FM	H	Short	Nose or Mouth?	Quiet	Insects Small verts.
Stenoderminae	FM	H	Short	Nose	Quiet?	Fruit
Glossophaginae	FM	H	vShort	Nose	Quiet	Fruit Nectar
Desmodontidae	FM	H	Short	Nose	Quiet	Blood
Noctilionidae	CF or mixed	P²	Short	Mouth	Loud	Fish Insects
Vespertilionidae	FM	P²	Short	Mouth[1]	Loud[1]	Insects
Molossidae	FM	P²	Short	Mouth	Loud	Insects

Notes: CF = constant frequency pulses; FM = frequency modulated pulses. For the search-phase pulses, short implies about 5 m sec; vshort about 1 m sec or less; long about 50 m sec.

[1] But *Plecotus* may emit either through the nose or the mouth and the pulses are quiet.

[2] The pure frequency sounds are presumably derived by suppressing the harmonics which might be present. In some instances indications of harmonics do appear in these bats' pulses.

ELECTRONIC BAT DETECTORS

In view of these characteristic sounds one is tempted to hope that an apparatus could be devised for field use which would detect, and perhaps identify, bats in flight. We can easily recognise the sounds produced by birds, so why not recognise bats from their cries? Despite assertions to the contrary, visual identification of flying bats is virtually impossible, so a reliable electronic bat detector would be a great asset in the field. Though full studies require complex equipment, even a simple detector could allow some check of whether wild bats behave as captive ones do.

A suitable instrument can be converted from a transistor radio, or an ultrasonic receiver purchased 'off the peg' for about £150 ($370). With the latter, the long ultrasonic pulses of horseshoe bats are rendered audible as a very distinctive series of yelps, or a continuous warbling if several are present. The frequency measurement on the tuning dial (83 or 119kHz) will tell us whether we are listening to a greater or lesser horseshoe bat. Noctule and pipistrelle are distinguishable by the quality of the sound, but the small *Myotis* species are difficult to distinguish from each other and long-eared bats are inaudible at more than a metre or so.

Despite its limitations, the bat detector can help to build up a general picture of bat distribution, with at least some indication of the species present (Hooper, 1966, 1969a, 1969b). By making nocturnal visits to parks for instance, Hooper has demonstrated that at least two species of bat (*Pipistrellus* and *Nyctalus*) still live in Central London, for instance, despite the absence of records from other sources for over twenty years. In countries with a more extensive bat fauna, individual recognition of species becomes even more difficult, but using a detector to make regular seasonal observations (perhaps combined with measurements of temperature and light intensity) could demonstrate differences in habits. In Canada, a Holgate ultrasonic receiver was used simply to count the number of 'passes' made by bats flying by and showed a significant decrease during rainstorms (Fenton, 1970). More activity was detected around habitations in rural areas than over undisturbed forest; more over lakes than beside streams or in fields.

EFFICIENCY OF BAT ECHOLOCATION

A rough indication of how good bats are at echolocation is given by weighing them before and after a known period of hunting. Dividing the weight-gain by the average weight of a prey animal will suggest the number of successful captures. This has in fact been done both in the field and under laboratory conditions. One individual *Myotis lucifugus* weighing 8.2g had swallowed 1.3g of insects in about 70 minutes' hunting time, and the average rate of insect accumulation for this species was about 1g per hour (Gould, 1955). Among similar examples for other species, an 18.9g *Eptesicus fuscus* had eaten 4g of insects in 90 minutes and a 5.3g *Pipistrellus subflavus* had consumed 1.4g in 30 minutes. To translate these weights into numbers of insects captured per hour requires some idea of the weight of individual prey items consumed. The smallest eaten by *Myotis lucifugus* were tiny gnats with a wing-span of only 3mm and weighing only 0.2mg, but larger items might have weighed about 3mg. If the average prey weighed 2mg, then the *Myotis* must have been catching 500 insects per hour. *Myotis lucifugus* released into a laboratory full of fruit flies (*Drosophila*, which do weigh about 2mg each), caught them at rates up to 1,200 per hour, or 1 every 3 seconds (Griffin, Webster and Michael, 1960). This rate of capture was determined primarily by the increase in weight of the bat over the hunting period, but was confirmed by the number of terminal-phase 'buzzes' recorded. Practically every chase must have been successful, and the experiment also rules out any suggestion that the bats might have been 'filter feeding' by flying through dense swarms of insects with their mouths open.

Such studies show how effective a bat's echolocation system is for catching insects, and from the bat's point of view this is obviously an important criterion. For a scientific evaluation of its efficiency rather more objective tests are obviously needed. One of the most widely used, and one which allows a comparison of the ability of different bats, is the wire-screen test: the bat has to fly a number of times through a loose screen of vertical wires or rods, and each passage through the screen is counted as a miss, a hit or a touch. The diameter of the wires can be varied and also their layout, so that the bat does not get used to their position. The wires are usually spaced slightly further apart than the size of the bat's wingspan, providing a barrier which it ought to miss by chance only about 35 per cent of the times it tries to fly through. Even with very thick wooden or metal bars, bats do not achieve 100 per cent misses in such tests, though their 'failures' under such conditions are usually only light touches and indicate carelessness or misjudgement. They certainly do not mean that the bats cannot detect the obstacles, for wires as thin as 0.28mm diameter are avoided on 89 per cent of flights by certain skilful *Myotis lucifugus*. (Such wires are only slightly thicker than 5amp fuse wire, 0.22mm diameter.) With thinner wires, success is reduced, wires of 0.07mm diameter being missed on only 35 per cent of flights, about the chance level.

With the fruit bat *Rousettus*, the ability to avoid wires (in complete darkness) falls below 70 per cent with wires of about 1mm diameter or less, so that it is evidently less proficient than the Microchiroptera. Indeed greater horseshoe bats can avoid wires as thin as 0.08mm diameter (the thickness of a human hair) on over 50 per cent of flights, even when the wires are only half a wing-span apart. Still more remarkable, *Megaderma lyra* (which it will be recalled is a 'whispering bat', using very faint signals) also proved capable of avoiding wires of only 0.08mm diameter. Finding that an ordinary barrier of such thin wires was no serious obstacle for them, Möhres (1967) tested them flying through a grid of vertical and horizontal wires. The squares were only 14cm across, so that the bats with their 40cm wing-span had to furl their wings almost completely to get through; yet they did not even slow down for the barrier (as *Rhinolophus* does) but shot through 'like missiles'.

Experiments of this sort enable some estimate to be made of the distance over which bats can detect prey or barriers by echolocation. As in the hunting procedures, the pulse-repetition rate changes from the slow search phase, as a bat approaches a barrier, to a terminal-phase buzz. Obviously the bat has detected the barrier by the point at which the pulse rate starts to rise; it is quite possible that it had detected the barrier earlier, so the distance from the point of change to the barrier gives a minimum estimate for the effective range of the system. *M. lucifugus* hunting fruit flies in the laboratory showed a change from search to approach phase between 23 and 83cm from the flies, and moreover could detect them anywhere within a cone of about 120° ahead. With the wire barrier it seemed as though the bats were responding as much as 200cm away (Griffin, Webster & Michael, 1960, Griffin, 1958). Möhres found *Rhinolophus*, with its beamed sound, reacting as much as 10 metres away from a barrier, while the quieter *Megaderma* probably detected barriers only within 2 metres range.

One special case of interest is the fish-eating bat, *Noctilio leporinus*. It can feed on insects, but as already seen fish form its usual diet and to catch these it flies very low over water, occasionally dipping in its enormous hind feet armed with sharp claws, which in flight point forward, so acting as a gaff. Observations of hunting *Noctilio* suggest that they did not just dip their feet at random, nor drag them 'hopefully' for long periods at a time, yet there were no evident ripples or protruding fins to suggest that the bats were responding to surface disturbances by the fish. Could *Noctilio* echolocate completely submerged fish? The difficulty with such a suggestion is that sound does not travel well from one medium to another. Of sound energy striking the water surface, 99.9 per cent would be reflected and only 0.1 per cent transmitted; any echo returning from a fish would suffer the same loss and become too faint to detect (Griffin, 1958).

This problem has been resolved by Suthers' (1965) experiments with captive *Noctilio*. These were trained to take cubes of fish meat attached to vertical wires mounted in a pool in the floor of their flight cage. Completely submerged fish cubes were only hit twice in over 600 attempts, a score which was probably achieved by random dipping. The swim bladders of submerged fish (which, containing air, might produce stronger echoes than the bodies of the fish alone) were simulated by tying small balloons beside the fish cubes, but the bats could not detect these either, so long as they were completely submerged. By contrast, when a submerged piece of fish was marked either by a wire (0.35mm diameter) projecting just 5mm above the surface, or by a small upwelling of water from a hose pipe beneath the surface, the bats dipped at it during 80–90 per cent of their trials. Evidently *Noctilio* reacts to small surface disturbances, but cannot detect completely submerged fish.

Suthers went on to test the ability of *Noctilio* to discriminate between different markers. They were able to distinguish a single wire, 1.3mm thick, from two wires each 0.9mm thick and placed 2cm apart (all projecting just 5mm above the water surface) with greater than 80 per cent success, though the strength of the echo from these two targets should have been similar. But they were unable to distinguish a projecting wire 11mm long and 1.34mm in diameter sloping north from a similar wire pointing south. These targets should have provided echoes of exactly the same strength and pattern, with one being a mirror image of the other.

This last test is a rather artificial one—natural targets of interest to bats do not generally differ only by sloping north or south! Nevertheless in other, equally artificial, tests bats do manage to show remarkable discrimination. Griffin, Friend & Webster (1965) devised a 'mealworm gun' which lobbed mealworms into the path of a flying bat. Skilful individuals managed after about a week's training to catch consistently 80–100 per cent of the larvae thrown near them. Mealworms are about 3mm in diameter and around 20mm long; in 'flight' they can either be stretched out or somewhat curled, so their echo patterns must vary. The next stage of the experiment was to interpolate between the mealworms plastic discs of 3mm thickness and either 12.5 or 16mm diameter; seen side-on these would be about the same thickness and length as a mealworm. Initially the bats tended either to catch nearly all the mealworms and the discs, or to avoid both, yet after about ten days, they had learnt to differentiate sufficiently well to take 80–100 per cent of the mealworms but only 10 to 20 per cent of the discs.

One other remarkable property of the bats' echolocation system is its resistance to jamming. Our own sense of hearing is susceptible to interference; it is difficult to hold a telephone conversation if someone nearby is talking loudly. Griffin and others subjected *M. lucifugus* and the long-eared bat *Plecotus townsendii*, which were undergoing the wire-barrier test, to various frequencies of sound, both pulsed and continuous and at levels far louder than any echoes the bats could be using. These attempts at jamming had no effect on the bats' ability to dodge the wires.

However, when 'white' or 'thermal' noise (random noise covering a wide range of frequencies) was used, the bats were evidently troubled, being most reluctant to fly at all. Yet if they were forced to fly, the *Myotis* still managed to dodge wires of 0.28mm diameter as successfully as before. With the *Plecotus*, which produce much weaker pulses, there was a sharp reduction in ability; wires missed on 69 per cent of flights in silence were missed on only 50 per cent of trials in the presence of intense white noise. Calculations suggest that the echoes of its own pulses were five decibels quieter than the surrounding noise and in theory the bat should not have been able to hear them at all. (It is supposed that a sound must be between 1 to 10 decibels louder than another to be heard above it.)

ANATOMY AND PHYSIOLOGY OF ECHOLOCATION

Naturally, since Microchiroptera rely on echolocation they show a number of anatomical and physiological specialisations in both the system transmitting sounds and the one for receiving echoes. Basically these are not very different from the appropriate systems in any other mammal, but since the specialisations go some way toward explaining the remarkable abilities of these bats they are well worth study.

Transmission

We have already mentioned that the ultrasounds of all Microchiroptera are vocal, produced in the larynx. This is relatively much bigger than in other mammals and in particular the cricothyroid musculature (fig 30) is very large. Most of the muscles of the

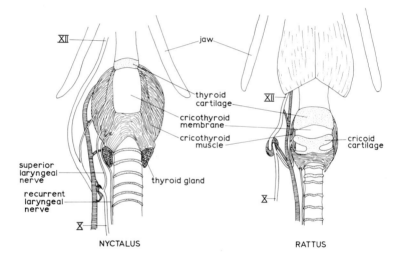

NYCTALUS   RATTUS

Fig 30. The larynx of *Nyctalus* (noctule bat) and of *Rattus* (laboratory rat). The distance between the jaws in these diagrams is the same—the larynx of the bat is relatively much larger, occupying about three-quarters of this width, compared with about one-third in the rat. The nerves which supply the laryngeal muscles in the bat are labelled with Roman numerals indicating the vagus (Xth) and hypoglossal (XIIth) cranial nerves.

larynx are innervated by the recurrent laryngeal nerve (a branch of the vagus nerve). Cutting this nerve usually causes serious interference with sound production—in man, normal speech becomes impossible. In the bats, however, severance of the nerve fails to interfere with the echolocation pulses, because the bats' enlarged cricothyroid muscles are controlled instead by the superior laryngeal nerve (another branch of the vagus). Cutting *this* nerve reduces the frequency of the emitted pulse from its usual ultrasonic level to an audible squeak (Novick & Griffin, 1961). Evidently the function of the cricothyroid muscles is to maintain high tension in the laryngeal membranes (bats do not have vocal cords as such), and the vibration of these taut membranes produces the ultrasonic sound as exhaled air is blown across them. These experiments affect the sound frequency but not its duration or strength, the control of which has not been investigated. Since bats do not use their ribs or intercostal musculature for respiration as we do, the puffs of air which must pass through the larynx are probably controlled by the muscular diaphragm.

In many bats the sounds produced in the larynx are emitted straight through the mouth which seems to lack special modifications associated with this. The Chilonycterinae have flaps of skin around the mouth which are puckered into a megaphone when (but only when) the bats are emitting. In other families, the nose leaf around the nostrils acts in part as a megaphone.

Reception

The reception mechanism includes the ears and the auditory centres of the brain associated with them. As in other mammals the ears consist of three anatomically distinct parts which we may consider in succession, the outer, middle and inner ears.

The *outer ear* consists of the ear flap, or pinna, and the tube, the auditory meatus, leading down to the tympanic membrane (ear drum). In the fruit bats the pinna is unremarkable, even that of the echolocating *Rousettus* being much like any other mammal, but in the Microchiroptera, the pinna is as variable as the nose leaf (except that it is never absent!). In many vespertilionids and phyllostomids (particularly nectar-feeding Glossophaginae) the pinna is fairly simple though large; many whispering bats have very large ears, (about as long as the body in *Plecotus*), and the two pinnae meet across the top of the head. Many bats have a small accessory lobe of skin, the tragus, which appears to stand sentinel in the middle of the pinna (and remains standing in *Plecotus* when the rest of the ear is folded away). The tragus is present in all Vespertilionidae (which lack any nose leaf) but absent in the Rhinolophidae, and it used to be suggested by European mammalogists that perhaps the functions of the tragus and horseshoe were analogous. It is now obvious that this is not so and in any case many bats (eg Megadermatidae, Phyllostomidae) have both tragus and nose leaf. One obvious function of the pinna is to collect up sound, rather like an ear trumpet, but vespertilionid bats manage to echolocate quite successfully when the pinnae (tragus included) have been amputated: the ear seems to suffer only a moderate (5 to 10 decibel) loss of sensitivity.

A more likely function for both pinna and tragus seems to be in determining the direction from which echoes are coming. Bats' ears are most sensitive, not to sounds returning from straight ahead but to sounds coming from about 35° to the side and 30° below the line of flight. Cutting off the tragus makes the ear 10 decibels less sensitive to sounds coming from below and less responsive to the precise direction of the sound source. Interference with the pinna can produce similar effects; in *Plecotus*, just glueing the two ears together can make one ear 10 decibels more sensitive and the other 15 decibels less, reducing success in the wire barrier test from 97 per cent to 62 per cent.

Finally, we should mention a peculiarity of the Rhinolophidae and Hipposideridae. When these bats emit a pulse, one pinna moves forwards and the other backwards and on the next pulse these movements are reversed. The function of this rapid ear waggling is unknown, but the Chilonycterinae, which also use constant-frequency pulses, seem to be doing something similar by nodding their heads in flight. Perhaps the movements assist in estimating distance or direction.

The mammalian *middle ear* consists of the tympanic membrane, a tight web of skin which vibrates when sound waves strike it, and a chain of three bones which carry these vibrations to the inner ear. Of the ear ossicles, the malleus is partly embedded in the tympanum, so picks up the vibrations directly. These are transmitted to the incus, then on to the stapes, the other end of which sits in the oval window of the inner ear. All three bones are lightly built in bats. The whole of the middle ear is covered by a dome formed from the tympanic bone, which also provides a C-shaped support for the tympanic membrane. The chain of bones forms a lever system magnifying the force transmitted between the malleus and stapes by 3 to 5 times. A second magnification effect results from the area of tympanum being between 16 and 53 times larger than the area of the stapes footplate (Henson, 1970), so that faint sounds detected by the tympanum become concentrated on a much smaller area.

There is one other important component of the middle ear: two small muscles, the stapedius and the tensor tympani, attached to the stapes and malleus respectively. Both these pull roughly at right angles to the line along which the bones transmit vibrations, so their function is one of damping rather than accentuating sound. In Microchiroptera, although the bones are slight, these muscles are particularly large, occupying for instance 0.25 cubic millimetres in *Plecotus* and as much as 0.55 cubic millimetres in the free-tailed bat *Tadarida brasiliensis*, but only 0.09 cubic millimetres in a small shrew of similar body weight. We have noted that echolocation pulses are often loud, and there is a danger that the bat could be effectively deafened by its own voice: the role of the two middle-ear muscles is to contract just as the bat emits its pulse, temporarily diminishing the sensitivity of the ear.

Now in FM bats, a search-phase pulse only lasts about 5msec and the muscles take 10msec to contract, implying that they would be too late. In fact they start to contract at the same time as the laryngeal muscles, 10msec before the pulse is actually emitted, and are therefore fully tense during emission. They have relaxed again about 5msec after the end of the pulse, so that the ear is then fully receptive to faint echoes. During a terminal-phase 'buzz', the pulses are in such quick succession that there is not time for the muscles to keep contracting and relaxing and they remain contracted throughout. The bat is of course close to its target by then and the echoes are loud enough to be perceived anyway. In bats using CF pulses, the timing of the middle-ear muscle contraction is not quite the same, as the constant-frequency part of the pulse coincides with the start of contraction, but the muscles are fully contracted during the terminal FM part of the pulse. There is a similar automatic response by our own middle-ear muscles when we speak, which may be one reason why we have difficulty hearing someone who tries to talk while we are talking ourselves.

The *inner ear* of mammals contains two sets of sense organs, one concerned with orientation (balance and acceleration), the other, the cochlea, concerned with hearing. The whole assembly is tightly encased in the periotic bone, perhaps to prevent outside pressure movements (for instance from the jaw muscles) from interfering with it. In bats the periotic and tympanic bones are tightly fused to each other, but almost completely isolated from the rest of the skull. Bone is quite a good sound-conductor and this separation may prevent the transmission of noise through the skull bones, so keeping sounds which enter one ear separate from those entering the other. It should certainly prevent noises travelling direct from the mouth to the ear.

The cochlea is a spirally coiled tube, inside which the vibrations set up by the stapes footplate vibrating in the oval window are translated into electrical impulses which can travel up the auditory nerve, to be interpreted by the brain. Not surprisingly, the cochlea is large in Microchiroptera, 20mm long in *Rhinolophus*, if straightened out (it is only 32mm long in a man, who is over 2,500 times heavier than the bat!), and spiralling through 3.5 turns. The detailed anatomy of the cochlea is rather complicated, but the important point is that a thin basilar membrane runs almost its full length, and on this rest the actual sensory cells. Each of these has little trigger-like hairs which can be distorted by vibrations in the membrane causing electrical changes in the sensory cells, which in turn generate impulses in the auditory nerve. It is not clear (in any mammal) exactly how the cells along the basilar membrane are arranged so that they respond to particular noises, but it is known that the tip of the cochlea is more responsive to low-frequency sounds and the basal region (nearest the oval window) to high frequencies; it is the basal region that is especially large in bats.

The presence of a small opening (the round window) has enabled physiologists to implant small electrodes in the cochlea of anaesthetised bats, to record the tiny electrical changes which result when the cochlea responds to a sound. The records obtained, cochlear microphonic potentials or CM potentials, may result directly from the distortion of the hair cells; certainly they correspond exactly with what the ear receives. This technique has proved very useful; for a start it has been possible to demonstrate that bats' ears do indeed respond directly to sounds of ultrasonic frequencies, in fact to any frequency from 1kHz to 100kHz (in *Tadarida* and *Myotis*). Recordings of CM potentials were used to show that the maximum sensitivity of the ear was to sound from the side, rather than straight ahead.

The Brain

Part of the mid-brain called the inferior colliculus is directly concerned with hearing. In most Microchiroptera these colliculi (one each side) are, as you would expect, very large, forming 14 to 23 per cent of the brainstem. In Megachiroptera, they form no more than 8.5 per cent, even in the echolocating *Rousettus*. In many Microchiroptera the colliculi are so big that they form bulges on the dorsal surface of the brain; this has enabled physiologists to plant electrodes on them and record the electric potentials arriving at the brain as well as those in the cochlea. Recordings can be taken from the inferior colliculus of an active bat and Henson (1967) has even managed to get records from *Chilonycteris* in flight. These show the pattern of electrical response in the brain in re-

167

lation to the emitted pulses and confirm that the outgoing pulse usually produces a rather faint response. The echoes, on the other hand, produce a succession of strong potentials (fig 31), four to each echo; these are referred to as the N_1, N_2, N_3, and N_4 responses, from the order in which they appear.

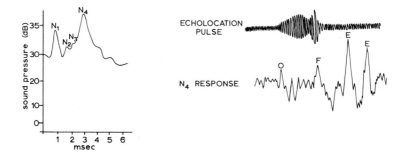

Fig 31. Electrical response of the brain of *Chilonycteris*. The graph, left, shows what is picked up by an electrode placed on the inferior colliculus of the brain after an echolocation pulse is emitted, or an echo heard, at a pressure of 30 decibels. The first (N1) response occurs only 1msec later and indicates the arrival of a 'message' in the auditory nerve. Two minor responses (N2, N3) are followed after 3.5msec by the major (N4) response. On the right are simultaneous records from an oscillograph of the echolocation pulse and the N4 response of the brain of a flying *Chilonycteris*. The brain responds to the beginning ('on'—O) of the pulse, to the FM sweep at the end (F) and to two echoes producing much bigger responses. (After Henson, 1970.)

The discovery that the bat's brain responds more strongly to an echo than to the emitted pulse is obviously significant when one tries to interpret how echolocation works. There are at least four different ways in which a bat may seem to hear echoes more clearly than other sounds. We have already noticed that the ear has directional variations in sensitivity, responding most to sounds coming from 35° to the side. The activity of the middle-ear muscles, suppressing the reaction to the outgoing pulse, is also important in some bats. Some brain cells seem to be 'tuned' to specific frequencies, and this will of course fit them well to hearing echoes of those frequencies. Finally, records of the electric potentials in some nerve cells show that they respond more to a second pulse of a given frequency than they do to the first. The outgoing pulse constitutes such a first sound and the echo is a second sound which will, at least in FM bats, cover the same frequencies. This mechanism will obviously enhance the perception specifically of echoes, and seems likely to be a specialisation of the brains of echolocating mammals. In humans, by contrast, echoes are selectively eliminated by the brain—that is, nerve cells respond less to a second sound of the same frequency than to the first.

WHAT DO THE BATS HEAR?

To understand what the bats might be listening to in the echoes they receive we need to bear in mind some of the characteristics of sound itself. In particular, the speed of sound, its attenuation, reflectivity and Doppler shift are likely to be useful features to bats.

Speed of sound
Since sound normally travels in air at a constant speed of about 340mm/msec, the time an echo takes to return from an object to a bat will itself indicate distance. Moreover, the CF bats, with their long 50msec pulses, will be informed of any object which is within 8.5 metres of them, since they will receive the first echoes from it before they finish emitting the pulse $\frac{(340 \times 50)}{2}$ mm $= 8.5$m). However, two objects 1 centimetre apart but one behind the other will return echoes separated by only 0.03msec, and it seems unlikely that the brain could resolve such small time differences. Yet it is known from training experiments that bats can somehow discriminate between such closely spaced objects. Since the ears of a small bat are only about 1cm apart, it is also unlikely, though possible, that the bat could detect the arrival of an echo at the nearest ear fractionally earlier than at the other.

169

Attenuation

Sound intensity diminishes with the square of the distance, so that an echo from an object 3 times as far away as another similar one will be 81 times as faint. In addition to this 'spreading loss', the air itself causes some attenuation, part of the sound energy being lost in agitating the air molecules. This effect is more significant with high frequency sounds; at 55kHz, for example, about 2dB are lost for every metre the sound travels. In recording N_4 potentials from the brain, an increase of only 1–2dB in the strength of the sound played at the ear can result in a change at the brain from practically no response to almost maximum response. In other words, a bat's hearing is very sensitive to variations in the amplitude of sound; indeed changes of only 0.1–0.2dB produced different reactions in the brain. In the experiments with *Noctilio* distinguishing between single and double wires, Suthers (1965) found that the single wires reflected echoes which were consistently 1–2dB louder than the peak echoes from the double wires. Moreover, the strength of the echo from the single wire was constant all round, while the double wires gave strong echoes in some directions, weak in others. Different targets would produce comparable differences and there is obviously scope here for discrimination by the bats.

Finally, we may recall the marked directional sensitivity of the ear, with maximum response to a sound coming from 35° to the side. Obviously an echo from 35° to the left of a bat would produce maximum effect in its left ear, but a very low response in its right ear. In *Tadarida*, an echo with a frequency of 60kHz could differ as heard in the left and right ears, by as much as 60dB. During the attempts to mask the echolocation of *Myotis* and *Plecotus* with 'white noise', it was noticed that under very bad conditions the bats started to fly zigzag courses, probably in an effort to hear their echoes from the wires in directions of maximum sensitivity while minimising the noise from the loudspeakers. It is presumed that the combination of this behaviour and the directionality of the ears helped overcome the interference and was responsible for them doing better than seemed theoretically possible.

Reflectivity

Just as surfaces can be shiny, reflecting lots of light, or matt, reflecting little, so they can reflect much or little sound. The most important feature of a surface from this point of view is its size relative to the wavelength of the sound. Objects smaller than the wavelength scatter the sound rather than reflect it, while objects larger than the wavelength reflect it well. This has important repercussions for a bat interested in catching small insects. A lesser horseshoe bat using a frequency of 119kHz produces wavelengths about 3mm long, while the larger *Rhinolophus ferrumequinum* emitting at 83kHz produces wavelengths of 4mm. Perhaps *R.hipposideros* can detect insects only 3mm long which *R.ferrumequinum* overlooks. The possibilities for a frequency-modulating bat are even more intriguing—in sweeping from 90kHz down to 50kHz, it will raise the minimum size of insect which it should readily detect from 4mm to 7mm—smaller insects will produce echoes to the start of the FM pulse but apparently disappear toward the end!

Doppler shift

When a bat is flying towards an object, an echo does not have to travel as far as an outgoing pulse, simply because of the distance the bat has flown between emitting the pulse and hearing the echo. In other words, the sound apparently returns faster than it went. But we have noted that the actual speed of sound in air is constant, and this apparently faster return is heard as a change in frequency, known as the Doppler shift. The distance between the bat and the object decreases as the bat flies towards it, the wavelengths in that space are compressed and shorter wavelengths mean higher frequencies. Conversely, a bat flying away from an object would receive its echoes at lower frequencies. This obviously suggests a rather sensitive way of detecting flying insects— an insect flying away from the bat at the same speed as the bat will produce no Doppler effect, but one flying towards the bat will produce a very marked shift to a higher frequency.

This principle is perhaps not much use to an FM bat, for in sweeping through its range of frequencies it will in any case receive a variety of echoes. On the other hand, the CF bats, such as *Rhinolophus* and *Chilonycteris*, are evidently well equipped to perceive Doppler shifts. The long pulse certainly overlaps with many of the returning echoes, and since it is of constant frequency it provides a base against which a Doppler-shifted echo can be compared. A horseshoe bat converging with an insect at 10m/sec (ie each flying at 5m/sec) would hear the echo of its 83kHz pulse at about 88kHz. Neuweiler (1970) has shown that the ear of a horseshoe bat is remarkably *in*sensitive to the typical frequency of its pulses (which is presumably one reason why it doesn't deafen itself with its own cries) but very sensitive to frequencies only 0.5kHz either side of it. The same feature is found in *Chilonycteris* (Pollack *et al.*, 1972). Further, there is quite convincing evidence that horseshoe bats do indeed use Doppler shift (Schnitzler, 1968). Although they usually emit on a constant, typical, frequency, a *Rhinolophus* echolocating a swinging pendulum alters the frequency of its emission to compensate for the swing, so that the echo is heard at a constant frequency *despite* the movement of the pendulum.

There is evidently a wealth of information contained in the echoes of the pulses emitted by bats, and there is also plenty of evidence that their ears and the auditory centres of their brains are well attuned to these echoes. At present it is not clear just which bits of the information the bats use, and current research is much concerned with this point. The CF bats use Doppler shifts to gain information, but what in that case is the role of the terminal FM part of their pulses? For the FM bats the intensity, the loudness, of the echoes is important at least for indicating the position of a target.

Some recent studies by Bradbury (1970) provide an instructive example of the sort of experiments which are needed and also warn us that a simple answer is not to be expected. Bradbury constructed a sphere and a spheroid of the same material and of sizes that would produce echoes of closely similar amplitude. The sphere and the spheroid were suspended on either thin (0.28mm) or thick (0.35mm) strings, and tests beforehand showed that with the thicker strings the targets produced their strongest echoes at different frequencies. On the thinner strings the two targets produced very similar echoes. Bradbury used the large South American bat *Vampyrum spectrum*; two of them were very good at distinguishing between the targets on the large strings, scoring better than 70 per cent correct choices. Further tests with the targets on thin strings, however, showed that while one of them could no longer tell the difference, the other one still could. Evidently one of them relied upon differences in frequency, no longer present with the thin strings, while the other was using some other clue. The calibration tests showed that in a wide approach to the targets the sphere produced rather stronger echoes overall, which is probably what the other individual relied on, particularly as it tended to use a wider approach. If two individuals of the same species can use different means of assessing the same targets by echolocation, we can expect the differences between species to be much more difficult to understand and investigate.

CHAPTER 8

BATS AND MAN

In some ways bats have proved helpful to man. On the other hand they can become, by virtue of sheer numbers, a genuine economic pestilence, one of the reasons for the tradition of persecution from which they have suffered for centuries. Deliberate destruction and a host of indirect pressures have resulted in observed declines in temperate-zone species. This in turn has given rise to a new aspect to the interrelation of bats and man: the attempt to protect and conserve dwindling populations.

MAN'S USES OF BATS

The sinister association of bats with evil goes hand in hand with their most ancient employment in human affairs: as essential ingredients of sorcery and magic, where their contribution is usually seen as wholly malevolent. Paradoxically, in the allied fields of witchcraft and pseudomedicine they are often considered beneficial, their blood, hearts and hair being regarded as particularly potent for making both medicine and mischief. Various bat preparations were thought to give strength and cure rheumatism; consumption of roast bat was even supposed to stop children eating dirt! Bat dung was supposed to possess strong healing properties, and doubtless Macbeth's prognosticatory potions would have been less efficacious had his witches lacked the wool of bat to add to the other ingredients necessary for the correct casting of horoscopes. The absurdity of all this mumbo jumbo is compounded by frequent total contradictions; for example, that the fat of *Pteropus* cures baldness, but fat from other bats may be employed as a depilatory agent.

Today bats are still used in medicine, though happily not as a pharmaceutical ingredient; their modern role is as experimental tools. The transparency of the bat's wing permits a microscopic study of wound-healing in a living animal. The same property reveals details of blood circulation in the vessels of the wing; movement of blood cells and dyes are clearly visible, and the rates at which drugs are eliminated from the body can be measured. Even the effects of inhaled cigarette smoke on the peripheral circulation have been studied, again easier in the bat wing than in less translucent animal tissues.

There has been considerable research on the physiological mechanisms of hibernation in bats and other mammals. Understanding the control and effects of hypothermia is important, since many major surgical procedures are now carried out on humans at reduced body temperatures, when the body is less susceptible to damage and requires less oxygen. Investigators have also shown that during hibernation animals may age more slowly and they are more resistant to ionising radiation. Both factors could become important in deferring human senility, and might even be essential if space travel, involving journeys lasting many years, is ever to become a feasible proposition.

Discovery of the bats' ability to detect objects in total darkness prompted experiments aimed at providing blind people with an echolocation system. Practised people can interpret patterns of echoes resulting from noises they themselves create. Providing such people with narrow-beam ultrasonic-sound generators (used to scan the surroundings like a 'sound torch') and a suitable detector enabled them to behave like bats, feeling their way about sonically without producing audible sounds to annoy other people. An ultrasonic system also has the advantage of being little affected by potentially confusing ambient noise. Early work coupling bat sensory systems with the problems of the blind is described by Griffin (1960), and includes many simple experiments which help considerably in understanding the properties and potential of reflected sound as a means of guidance.

Carrying development work for the blind several stages further, Kay (1967) reported the testing of very sophisticated 'sound spectacles' which direct a wide beam of ultrasonics in front of the head and detect the echoes with two receivers in the position of the ears. Moving the sound source and both detectors with the head is similar to the system used by many bats, and the resultant Doppler-shift effects help to increase the amount of information gained from the system.

Future work on bats may reveal how they use reflected sound patterns, not just to detect objects but also discriminate between shapes and textures. The bat may still hold the key which could unlock the door to a wider world for the blind, with enhanced perception of what the rest of us take for granted. The technology of radar may also benefit from further study of bat echolocation systems, particularly from species (like *Plecotus*) that can recognise, apparently from echoes alone, a stationary insect on a static background of similar density. There is much to learn for despite spectacular developments in electronic gadgetry we still cannot reduce the size of even a simple radar system to the dimensions of a whole bat let alone just its ears and brain. Future studies on special features of bat biology may help extend man's own biological capabilities. The mechanisms of sperm storage and delayed fertilisation (Chapter 5) are already relevant to livestock breeding and, with future population growth and increased popularity of vasectomies, may become of more direct personal concern to us all.

Most of the more important 'uses' of bats are indirect, the benefit to man being derived from the bat's role in maintaining diverse and balanced ecosystems. We have seen in Chapter 3 how certain species are valuable pollinators of forest trees. Others consume thousands of tons of insects every year; artificial bat roosts have been constructed in the effort to introduce bats to areas troubled by irritating or disease-carrying plagues of insects. But insect populations easily make good the bat depredations. Moreover, bats take almost exclusively nocturnal species, so may not select the species they have been imported to control; they do not breed rapidly, are susceptible to the poisons used against the insects and may themselves be carrying rabies—a disease worse than anything that the insects may transmit. Bats therefore seem inappropriate for the role of introduced biological control agents, although naturally occurring colonies may help in keeping down insects, for example harmful wood-boring beetles in house roofs, though the householder may not view their tenancy in this light.

The suggestion that bats be put on the menu would elicit almost unanimous revulsion, even in countries where gourmets delight in the consumption of snails, frogs' legs and live oysters. This may stem from the Biblical admonition (Deuteronomy 14 : 18) that God's people shall not eat any abominable thing including 'unclean birds' like owls, hawks and bats and 'every creeping thing that flieth'. Nevertheless some of the larger bats find favour as human food, and why not? The Megachiroptera feed on wholesome fruit and juices, are large (*Pteropus* may weigh 1kg, as much as a scrawny chicken and is a good deal more tender) and are said to be agreeable in taste despite the strong superficial odour from their skin glands. Surprisingly, bats are relished in many parts of the Old World tropics, yet not in tropical America. The absence of megachiropterans only partly explains this phenomenon, since several of the large numerous fruit-eating phyllostomids seem equally suitable as food.

In some parts of the world where bats form especially large colonies in caves, their accumulated dung has proved sufficiently voluminous to merit its collection as a commercial enterprise. One of us visited a 'guano mine' in Mount Suswa, Kenya, where a nursing colony of *Otomops* had produced a mound of dung over 3 metres high, into which one sank knee-deep at every step. The guano from insectivorous bats has a higher nitrate content than that produced by fruit-eating species, and the best deposits occur in dry caves where there is little water to leach out the nutrients. Usually guano collection is a small-scale operation for which no production records exist, but at the Carlsbad Caverns in New Mexico the dung from *Tadarida brasiliensis* occupied several hundred square metres to a depth of 15 metres or more and 100,000 tons of it were removed in the first forty years of this century.

Bat guano has mostly been used as fertiliser (you can even buy packets of it in the florists and supermarkets of Nairobi), but in the American Civil War guano was taken from caves in Texas and the nitrates extracted to make gunpowder. This was not the last time that bats found a use in warfare. In World War II, 'project x-ray' was conceived. The idea was to equip thousands of bats with small incendiary bombs and release them over hostile territory in the hope that they would seek shelter in houses, factories and ammunition dumps where their little napalm bombs would burn with a 50cm flame for eight minutes and initiate a thoroughly worthwhile destruction of enemy property. The chosen bats were *T. brasiliensis* because they were abundant and they could fly 10 to 15 miles with a bomb equivalent to their own weight. The US navy leased the necessary caves in Texas and marines were posted to guard them. Successful field tests were carried out, but the project was cancelled in 1944, not long after some bats had escaped with their bombs and, with poetic justice, set light to the project's headquarters!

KEEPING BATS IN CAPTIVITY

Because bats are useful in experimental laboratory work there is sometimes a need to maintain colonies of them in captivity. People may wish to keep them as pets and it is also fashionable for zoos to try and breed threatened species. In view of the difficulties involved in keeping most bats, to say nothing of the loss to wild populations and the disease risk, our considered advice is 'don't'. However, in a comprehensive book we should include a few words about the care of captive bats.

The Megachiroptera are relatively easy to keep, but need heated accommodation, (above 22°C) with a humid atmosphere. Microchiroptera are more troublesome especially the insectivorous species, mainly due to the problem of providing an adequate diet. Mealworms are expensive (pound for pound, dearer than caviar or smoked salmon!) and often difficult to get. A substitute 'bat glop' made from mashed banana, boiled egg, cottage cheese and vitamins can be used to supplement the supply of mealworms or other insect food. Vampires are surprisingly easy to keep; a weekly trip to the slaughterhouse will provide a supply of blood for them, but their living quarters need to be very warm. A full account of the art of keeping bats has been provided by Racey (1970 & 1972), but there are legal restrictions on the importation of bats and other rabies-susceptible animals.

BATS AS PESTS

As the natural pollinators of the wild progenitors of such useful trees as avocados, bread fruit, mango, banana and guava, bats have played an important part in assisting man's colonisation of the tropics, but an ungrateful *Homo sapiens* must now begrudge them the very fruits which they helped to provide! In the tropics, frugivorous bats do considerable damage to fruit plantations, especially attacking valuable soft fruits, but orchards are not their sole source of food. Flying foxes (*Pteropus* spp) in Australia were thought by Ratcliffe (1932) to feed primarily on fruits and blossoms growing wild in the forest; periodic depredations in orchards and plantations resulted from droughts and other natural difficulties which forced the bats to seek alternative food supplies. Perhaps because of their generally greater size, Old World pteropodids cause the greatest damage, but fruit-eating phyllostomids (eg *Carollia* and *Artibeus*) certainly contrive to make themselves a nuisance in tropical America.

In temperate latitudes, frugivorous bats would be unable to find sufficient sustenance for many months of the year. Parts of the United States, notably Florida and southern California, are technically temperate but sufficiently warm to support multi-million-dollar soft-fruit industries, so the importation of fruit bats into the USA is prohibited. In areas of the world already troubled by the depredations of frugivorous bats, efforts to frighten them away are sometimes successful. Nets and other obstacles can be expensive and are often ineffective: bats can eat peaches by sucking the soft flesh through the mesh of a protective net! Large-scale control measures concentrate on mass destruction of colonies. Bats have been decimated using guns, poisons, explosives or flame throwers, but the cost of such activities is not normally warranted by the amount of damage done by the bats.

Many species of bat could become minor pests if their numbers became excessive, as could any other animal, and their droppings and parasites could become notably troublesome. Indeed it is believed human bed bugs (*Cimex*) were originally derived from bats when both bats and man were cohabitors of caves.

Some bats normally live in great concentrations, where sheer numbers can constitute a problem; but the risk of being smothered by them or eaten alive by their parasites and scavengers is run only by visitors to their colonies! Local abundance of bats may pose a threat to low-flying aircraft. The huge Bracken Cave colony in Texas has the US Air Force as a neighbour, and at one time pilots flying sorties there after dark stood a one in nine chance of colliding with bats, risking serious damage to windscreen and engines. Fortunately dense bat swarms show up on radar screens.

As carriers of disease bats pose a more serious problem to the welfare of man, even in temperate regions. A great variety of viral, bacterial, protozoan and mycotic pathogens have been recorded from bats; many are harmless, some cause minor afflictions and one, the rabies virus, is almost 100 per cent fatal. As vectors of disease, bats should be taken especially seriously because they are a long-lived highly mobile group of mammals (Chapter 6), potentially capable of swiftly spreading infections far and wide.

Histoplasmosis is one of the diseases associated with bats, particularly in humid tropical regions. It is caused by a fungus (*Histoplasma capsulatum*) which normally lives in soil, but can produce infective spores. These may be inhaled, and result in a respiratory illness, only rarely fatal in man. The organism thrives best in soil with a high nitrogen content; heaps of bat guano are ideal. In some parts of the world, the local populace already have naturally acquired infections, with no detriment to their health. Elsewhere, strict avoidance of contact with bats and their dung may prevent infection, but since *Histoplasma* also lives in bird dung and even ordinary soil, exaggerated caution is pointless.

Bats have yielded 28 different types of virus, plus antibodies for 32 others (Constantine, 1970). Many of these viruses are specific to certain areas and of sporadic occurrence. The most serious causes rabies (hydrophobia), a disease caused by a virus that travels from the point of entry through peripheral nerves to the spinal cord and brain. Visible symptoms include fever, uncontrolled salivation ('foaming at the mouth') and acute spasms which eventually result in paralysis and a painful death. The disease is of course harboured by many mammals. It kills over 100 million dollars-worth of cattle annually in the Americas (50,000 head per year in Argentina alone), and prevents commercial stock-rearing over large areas of Central and South America.

The rabies virus reaches the salivary glands of an infected animal, multiplies there and can be passed to other warm-blooded hosts if they are bitten. The most serious vector among the bats is obviously the vampire, which bites many animals during its normal feeding activities, and harbours infective virus material for unusually long periods. Vampire-borne rabies was not actually proved to have affected man until 1931, though it was suspected as a cause of cattle deaths as much as 200 years earlier. As carriers of rabies vampires have been more intensively studied than most other bats; witness the fact that a partial bibliography for this species (Linhart, 1971) runs to 53 pages.

In Trinidad, antivampire squads follow up reports of cattle being attacked by the bats. One of us accompanied a team on several dark nights (vampires shun bright moonlight), and saw how the cattle were examined for fresh bites; then, with a cow tethered as 'bait', mist nets were set up in strategic positions and the bats were snared in the lower panels of the net as they flew close to the ground or scurried about seeking a victim. Their habit of returning to the site of the previous night's meal makes them easy to catch; all those visiting a particular farmstead could be eliminated without killing other species—or vampires which do not bother the farmer. Netting is hardly practicable over most of the vampires' range, where transport and communications are often poor. It is also time-consuming and therefore expensive: it cost about $10 for every vampire killed in Trinidad, and despite an annual toll exceeding 1,300 bats, there has been no evident decline in population size.

Bright lights and other devices may frighten away the bats, but cowsheds and other buildings can be made bat-proof with wire netting, though free-ranging herds remain at risk. Study of the vampire's behaviour has helped devise other means of control. Its habit of returning to a previous victim means that fresh bites on a cow can be surrounded by thick smears of syrup and strychnine mixture with a good chance of poisoning the bats when they come back. Greenhall (1963) reported killing twelve vampires in a few hours this way, and an earlier poisoning programme killed over 600 in three years. Exploiting the vampire's habit of mutual grooming (two or more bats lick and groom each other's fur), captured vampires can be smeared with a mixture of petroleum jelly and an anticoagulant, then released. Other bats attempting to groom their fur when they return to the roost will swallow the anticoagulant and soon die from internal bleeding. The 'stoolpigeon' bats remain a lethal threat to their solicitous companions until either the mixture or the remaining bats are all gone. Field trials with this technique in Mexico and Brazil reduced the number of vampire bites on cattle in some areas by 95 per cent, and suggested that the exercise need only be repeated once every five years or so in order to keep the vampires to a minimum.

If it is essential to control bats, then selective methods such as these are clearly preferable to indiscriminate use of gas and explosives which eradicate whole colonies which may include harmless species. Hundreds of caves have been blown up in Brazil, and at one time nearly a million assorted bats were gassed every year in Venezuelan roosts; a crude and wasteful saga of unnecessary habitat destruction.

The use of vaccines to eliminate rabies in South America is more expensive than vampire control, and anyway is hardly practicable. Brazil alone has 79 million cattle, many living as free-ranging herds in inaccessible regions. Vaccines may help contain a localised outbreak, but a complete vaccination programme is out of the question.

Vampires are the worst culprits because they habitually bite other animals, but in 1953 the rabies virus was found in insectivorous bats in Florida. Since then rabies has been detected in 26 out of 40 species of bat in the USA, in every state of the Union except Hawaii; and also in various insectivorous and frugivorous bats in South America. Although these other species do not normally bite people or large animals, the 'furious' form of rabies makes them bite indiscriminately. In the 'dumb' form of the disease the bat becomes moribund but is just as dangerous, since sick bats lying about may be picked up by people (especially children) out of curiosity or a desire to help. Constantine's report (1967b) that rabies could be contracted without a bite, just by breathing 'infected air', seems to add to the problem, but it is worth noting that by mid-1973 over 17 million people had toured the Carlsbad Caverns (whose bat colonies are known to have included rabid individuals) without detriment to their health.

Bat rabies seems to be becoming more prevalent. In 1972, forty-seven states in the USA reported bat-rabies occurrences, 41 per cent more cases than the average for the preceding 5 years. In Canada, another report (Beauregard, 1969) based upon examination of 628 insectivorous bats revealed that 44 (belonging to 7 species) were rabid, though none of the 22 people bitten by them contracted the disease.

In Europe, rabies is becoming increasingly prevalent in wild mammals, and in 1970 the British Government set up a Committee of Enquiry to review the situation. In its report (Anon, 1971) the Committee did not include bats in the list of probable sources of future outbreaks. Even though the 35km width of the English Channel would be well within the flight capabilities of many British bats (Chapter 6), the risk of their bringing rabies to Britain is minimal; smuggled pets constitute a far more serious threat. Over-reaction to a rabies outbreak, with massive persecution of wildlife, would in fact be liable to drive mobile species (like foxes and bats) into widespread dispersal, thus exacerbating the situation.

DECLINE AND CONSERVATION

Many people have the feeling that bats are less abundant these days, a view officially endorsed by scientists from twenty countries at the 1970 International Bat Research Conference in Amsterdam. They agreed that most temperate-zone species had declined in numbers, some to the point of extinction in certain areas, particularly in the United States.

Measuring population declines requires an accurate census, repeated at regular intervals, and this is difficult with bats, though species which congregate in caves during the winter can be counted fairly readily. Numbers of the most conspicuous British cave-dwelling bat, the greater horseshoe, can be estimated fairly reliably, since the majority of the population is centred on known caves in the south and west of the country: and this species has declined by 80 to 90 per cent in fifteen years (Racey & Stebbings, 1972). Probably only about 1,000 remain in Britain, most of these very vulnerable to the threats that have caused this drastic decline in numbers. Other British species like pipistrelles and noctules, which are not among the more vulnerable cavernicolous species, are still fairly abundant. The status of rare species is precarious and their future survival probably depends entirely upon protection of them and their roosts.

Where bats cause damage or spread disease, some form of control is justified, but in most places they do little or no harm, and the reasons for their persecution, and often total eradication, can be sickeningly trivial. Ideas about their damaging the massive stonework of old buildings are silly, and notions of 'evil' and witchcraft are surely more appropriate to a superstitious medieval society than our own. Many people are disturbed by bats squeaking in their roof and wish to dispose of them; the noisiest colonies are those containing babies which call lustily for their mother (just as human babies do); should they be killed for this? In any case nursing colonies are likely to disperse after a few weeks if left alone.

The idea that bats get tangled in peoples' hair dies hard. It has been suggested that the story originated when houses had no ceilings and baby bats falling from a colony in the roof could drop on to the heads of people below and cling there desperately. Certainly young bats do instinctively hang on tight, but adults are normally not likely to land on humans and it is actually quite difficult to get one to become tangled in hair even when it is given every assistance!

Bat colonies in houses are frequently exterminated (sometimes with official help) because they make a mess. Droppings accumulate on the floor or below a roost entrance, but they are only composed of compacted insect fragments representing no hazard to health and do not even smell, except in large heaps. Eradication of these colonies is usually done by igniting smoke generators in the roost, or puffing in poison gas. One man boasted of removing seven buckets-full of bats after gassing his roof: 1,500 bats found guilty and sentenced to death whilst unaware of the charge against them and given no chance to move elsewhere. Often unwanted bats could be caught for release elsewhere, but the easiest way to get rid of a bat colony is to block the roost entrance after they have flown out one evening (preferably not in early summer when young may be left inside). Repellents like creosote, mothballs and paradichlorbenzene may help keep the bats away if the roost cannot be sealed.

Attempts at the humane control of bats by scaring them away have met with limited success. The size of colonies in nine Canadian house roofs decreased by up to 90 per cent when they were subjected to constant illumination, whilst two unlit control colonies *increased* by 57 and 97 per cent respectively (Laidlow & Fenton, 1971). Lights are cleaner and safer for bats and people than poisons, but elimination is rarely justified on public health grounds in temperate regions; and control for purely aesthetic reasons should be weighed against the beneficial activities of bats.

The loss of roosts must hasten the decline of bat populations. Hollow trees are, almost by definition, old and often partially rotten. Nowadays relatively fewer trees are left to reach such a state and every one that is cut down is a loss to the bats. Similarly few old buildings are now left in poor condition for long; big old houses, with their enormous roof spaces and abundance of batworthy nooks, are torn down to be replaced by bungalows and maisonettes. Many colonies are destroyed accidentally as a consequence of fumigation to control the spread of beetle and fungus infections in roof timbers, especially in old buildings. Perhaps the most serious loss is that of caves, mines and other underground haunts. Such places are vital as hibernacula to the bats of large areas (Chapters 4 & 6), yet these holes in the ground are used for mushroom-growing, tourism, caving and dumping rubbish, or filled in by careful landowners.

Racey & Stebbings (1972) revealed that 42 underground roosts had disappeared in recent years in southern England, where for geological reasons such places are scarce anyway. Large-scale quarrying of limestone continually threatens the major areas of natural caves, and becomes more serious with increasing demands for cement.

Changing methods of land use have resulted in many areas of diverse plant life being replaced by crop monocultures. Hedgerows are removed, to the tune of several thousand miles per year; one English county, Huntingdonshire, lost 71 per cent of its hedgerows in 20 years. The intensification of agriculture, the spread of urbanisation, the proliferation of roads and the general 'tidying up' of the countryside (eg by draining ponds, piping ditches and removing 'weeds') combine to render habitats less suitable for bats and for the insects upon which they feed. Continued sampling at Rothampstead Research Station (Hertfordshire) revealed a 50 per cent decline in the numbers of flying insects during the period 1945–60.

Pollution and pesticides further diminish the bats' food supply. Aspects of bat biology make them far more vulnerable than most animals to poisoning by persistent pesticides: animals at the end of food chains, like bats, are likely to ingest small amounts of insecticide in the fatty tissues of their prey and in time may suffer seriously from this accumulated load. In a sample of 38 British bats (mostly *P. pipistrellus*), DDE, a metabolite of DDT, was present in every one; and the general level of contamination was higher than that reported for insectivorous and carnivorous birds (Jefferies, 1972). Bats would be especially liable to accumulate large organochlorine residues because they consume a lot of food in proportion to their own weight, often hunt over agricultural areas and live a long time.

Pesticide residues in body fat are relatively harmless, but when fat reserves are utilised the organochlorine compounds are released into the blood stream. During the autumn a bat may therefore sow the seeds of its own destruction as it accumulates fat whose organochlorine content will be released into the body over winter, perhaps attaining lethal concentrations by the end of hibernation, as indeed Jefferies showed. In March, very high levels were detected: 34.7 parts per million, when laboratory tests indicate that as little as 45ppm can be lethal. This must add significantly to the risks that bats already face during the latter part of their hibernation period.

Experiments by Luckens & Davis (1964) on American bats (*Eptesicus fuscus*) have suggested that they are much more sensitive to DDT than any mammal previously tested. The 'LD_{50}' (dose rate lethal to 50 per cent of the experimental sample) was between 25 and 40mg/kg compared with 100–800mg/kg for rats, 175–450mg/kg for mice and up to 1,170mg/kg for rabbits. These experiments were conducted at the end of winter when the bats' pesticide content may already have been critical and additional experimental contributions could have been the 'last straw'. However, tests by Jefferies on pipistrelles in summer still revealed them to be more sensitive to DDT than other mammals, with an LD_{50} level of 63mg/kg.

Accumulation of pesticide residues has been blamed for the decline of many bird populations, and may similarly affect bats. One colony of guano bats, exceeding 25 million in 1963, was estimated to comprise only 30,000 in 1969 (Cochrum, 1970) and during 1968 there were reports of 'sick' bats dying by the hundred in many places in the USA. Sub-lethal poisoning may cause sterility; because of the bats' slow reproduction rate, the effects of this would not be immediately apparent and population recovery would take a very long time.

Sadly, one other proven cause of bat decline is the bat workers themselves, whose enthusiasm seems to have outstripped their good sense on occasions. Apart from the dangers of physical damage inflicted by poorly designed rings, we find that even reputable investigators such as Davis and Hitchcock (1965) report that 'aerosol insecticides and a granary fumigant were effective in flushing bats from their hiding places . . .'. To be fair, they did curtail the use of these after discovering that they were 'sometimes harmful to the bats', but that should have been obvious beforehand. In 1964 the American Society of Mammalogists passed a resolution condemning disturbance in roosts and the removal of bats for non-scientific purposes. Some 'scientific' investigations surely merit unreserved condemnation, like the one performed only a year later in which 140 bats were blinded, not by some reversible method, but by having their eyes burnt out with red-hot needles; a barbarity reported in the American Society of Mammalogists' own journal (Barbour *et al.*, 1966).

The effects of disturbance by bat investigators, especially during hibernation, may result in a population decline commencing almost immediately the study begins. The Dutch first noticed this in their long-term study in the South Limburg mines, finding 60 to 80 per cent decline in the numbers of lesser horseshoes and notch-eared bats between 1941 and 1956. They abandoned ringing these in 1955 and all species in 1957, but continued to census the bats in situ; the decline in numbers ceased almost immediately.

In Britain, Stebbings (1965) has shown that 5 visits per winter were sufficient to reduce the number of bats found by 50 per cent, even though they were not subjected to excessive disturbance. When interference, ringing especially, was minimised, by reducing visits to 1 per winter, the bat population increased over a period of 4 years (fig 32). Arousal from hibernation results in the loss of fat reserves, and if repeated can pose a serious threat to survival (Chapter 4). Stebbings' later observations on long-eared bats (1969) showed that those disturbed 6 times during hibernation lost the equivalent of 3 to 4 weeks' fat reserves as a result; an undisturbed bat could lose about 0.015g in 24 hours but if disturbed the loss increased to 0.58g. Even in summer, when energy expended could be easily recouped by feeding, disturbance still had a significant effect; numbers found on each visit diminished as bats retired to places where they could not be reached. Eventually only 50 per cent of them could be found.

The use of bats in short-term and poorly supervised school and university field-study projects should be discouraged, and perhaps bat-ringing should be controlled so that, like bird-ringing, it is only undertaken by trained and licensed people.

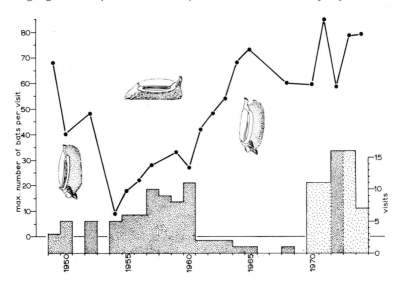

Fig 32. Disturbance by bat researchers can by itself cause serious declines in bat populations. Stebbings found that when he searched a small cave five or more times per winter, the highest number of bats found on any one visit dropped to about half and only recovered about four years after the number of searches was reduced. From 1970 the number of visits was increased, but bat disturbance was strictly controlled. In summer 1971 the cave was grilled to prevent casual visits, with some evident increase in the bat population. (Stebbings, 1969 & pers comm.)

Some bat species are more vulnerable than others, some may already be on the verge of extinction in many areas. If they are not to disappear completely, something must be done to conserve the remainder.

The legal protection of bats has already been effected in many countries (Austria, Bulgaria, Czechoslovakia, Denmark, East and West Germany, Finland, Hungary, Italy, Mexico, Poland, USSR, Yugoslavia and some states of the USA), usually as part of some comprehensive wildlife-protection legislation. In Britain, bats as a group are not protected; though there are serious penalties under the Protection of Birds Acts for molesting (sometimes even photographing!) any birds (except about twenty pest species). In 1973 a man was fined £75 and £150 costs for taking three kite eggs, yet there are more kites seen in Britain each year than the total of all the Bechstein's bats ever recorded there. The birds are strictly protected, but the bats could be killed with impunity.* Ideally legal protection should prevent casual destruction of bats, enable certain caves to be closed to visitors at least during winter, stop *uncontrolled* ringing and unsupervised 'scientific' studies, and assure the continuance of roosting sites where possible. It is appropriate that the pioneer location for European bat-population studies, the limestone mines in South Limburg, were in 1970 declared a protected reserve for bats by the Netherlands State Institute for Conservation Research. The mines cover an area of some 40sq km; ten species of bats have been recorded there during winter, and some 13,000 individuals have been banded since Bels began there the first large-scale bat-ringing programme in Europe in the 1930s. Carlsbad Caverns in New Mexico with their huge colonies of guano bats have also been fully protected, as a United States National Park, since May 1930.

Conservation, as opposed to mere protection, implies some active management, perhaps by providing roosts for bats. Specially constructed 'caves' would be costly, but most people with suburban gardens or young woodland could afford to build bat-boxes simulating tree-holes. These resemble bird nest-boxes, but with a slit entrance near the bottom rather than a round hole near the top. Experiments in Dorset with 20 boxes showed that some were visited within a few weeks, but it was 9 months before any were occupied continually, and 2 years before a breeding colony became established in one of them. In several European countries bat-boxes have been put up by the State forestry organisation in the belief that bats should be encouraged as potential controllers

* The Wild Creatures and Wild Plants Bill, reintroduced to Parliament in 1975, will, if passed, provide protection for some species.

of insects injurious to forestry interests. The main problem is that a box provides insufficient insulation and may have too dry an atmosphere.

Bat-boxes will not help cavernicolous species unless they have somewhere suitable to spend the winter. Roosts, as well as the bats themselves, must be legally protected. Holes in the ground attract inquisitive children and cavers, whose noise, smelly carbide and kerosene lamps and general disturbance is as destructive as many a deliberate form of bat persecution. The best method of protecting underground roosts is to fit a grille over the entrance, with spaces between the bars large enough to permit the entry of bats, but small enough to exclude humans, even persistent little boys!

In Britain, over two dozen sites have been grilled, and at all of them an increase in the bat population has been immediately evident. At least two roosts contained the highest winter population ever recorded there following the installation of grilles. The chief snag is that any obstruction at a cave entrance may impede air circulation and alter the subterranean microclimate. The changes effected may be very subtle, but the sensitivity of bats is such (Chapter 4) that the range of species inhabiting the place could be altered.

One design of grille uses 1 inch solid iron bars welded to angle-iron supports leaving 8in × 6in spaces, and cemented deep into the rock face around the cave entrance. A padlocked gate permits entry. This type has the advantage, particularly at large cave entrances, of doing little to obstruct the free passage of both bats and air, but is expensive and is finally only as strong as the hinges and lock on the gate. In soft rock it would also be difficult to prevent a determined vandal from digging his way round the edge of the grille.

Our own design, though unsuitable for large entrances, has no hinges; the gate consists of a set of parallel bars which slide away inside a reciprocal array of parallel pipes to permit authorised entry. The grille is fixed into position, then a section of sewer pipe is secured in front of it by a mass of scrap iron and concrete so that only a circular section of grille is accessible; its edges are protected by the concrete collar. The lock is only accessible by lying flat on one's back and reaching up and out of sight behind the concrete and sewer-pipe collar, again affording (we hope) some protection against surreptitious use of hacksaws.

In the end no protection, either physical or legal, will be completely effective without public understanding and sympathy. Bats are probably the most seriously threatened group of mammals in some countries, including Britain, and include some of the rarest terrestrial vertebrates. They are threatened at every stage of their life history: their insect food is diminishing and contaminated by insecticides; their breeding roosts suffer unwarranted disturbance and their specialised hibernation sites are rapidly disappearing. Yet, like the frogs and snakes, their lack of popularity ensures that their future can only get worse. Even those species that seek sanctuary in churches (often outnumbering human users of the building 100 to 1!) cannot expect much Christian charity from clergy obsessed by a few bat droppings but unaware that many bat species are down to their last few individuals.

Conservation has become a public issue, but efforts have been dangerously arbitrary, concentrating on animals with plenty of public appeal. We must not choose which kinds of wildlife we will permit to live based upon capricious concepts of prettiness or social acceptability! Bats are among the most interesting, complex and highly developed of all animals, as we have tried to show in this book; but in many places they need urgent help. They face decline, even extinction; against this sombre and very final threat our whims are trivial, our prejudices criminal.

CHAPTER 9

WHO'S WHO

This section provides a simple guide to the appearance, distribution and special features of the 17 families of bats. The first family, Pteropodidae, constitutes the whole of the sub-order Megachiroptera. All the other families are classified as Microchiroptera and are considered here with the most primitive family dealt with first.

Where sizes are given, 'length' refers to head and body and 'forearm' is the distance between elbow and wrist, which gives a more accurate guide to wing-size than trying to measure total wing-span. Nomenclature and approximate numbers of species follow Walker (1968).

Drawings for this section are based mainly on photographs in Walker and in the authors' own collection; distribution maps are based on Koopman (1970) and emphasise that bats are principally tropical animals with relatively few representatives in temperate regions. The maps each show the equator, both 'tropics', the Arctic circle and latitude 45° north and south.

An alphabetically arranged list of all the genera of bats, with the family to which each belongs, is found at the end of this chapter and may assist the reader to locate an unfamiliar bat.

TRUE FRUIT BATS ('FLYING FOXES') (fig 33)

Species: about 130 in 39 genera. The sole family of the Megachiroptera.

Major genera (8+ species): *Rousettus, Pteropus, Dobsonia, Epomophorus*; 21 other genera each contain only a single species.

Recognition: all have large eyes, no noseleaf and no tragus. The tail is small or absent and the uropatagium only rudimentary (fig 33A). All (except 5 minor genera) have a claw on the second finger as well as the usual claw on the thumb. The molar teeth are usually smooth and simple compared with the sharp jagged cusps (usually arranged in a 'W' pattern) on the molars of other bats. The palate is usually traversed by 8 prominent ridges, against which the tongue crushes soft food.

Size: the family includes the largest of all bats (*Pteropus* species), weighing 1,200g or more with a wingspan of up to 1.7 metres. There are also plenty of small pteropodids, weighing as little as 15g, dwarfed by many Microchiroptera.

Pteropodids feed mainly on fruit and juices, though the long-snouted sub-family Macroglossinae are specialised for nectar and pollen feeding. When at rest, the wings are often used to enclose the body. Though hanging head downwards, the long axis of the head is held at right angles to the body (most other bats hang with the face pointing directly downwards).

Except for *Rousettus*, fruit bats navigate visually and lack the complex neural and behavioural mechanisms associated with ultrasonic echolocation found among the Microchiroptera. This family from the Old World tropics are all basically rather similar in appearance; extreme forms include the long-nosed *Macroglossus*, the hammer-headed *Hypsignathus* and *Nyctimene* whose nostrils form a transverse tube across the end of the snout.

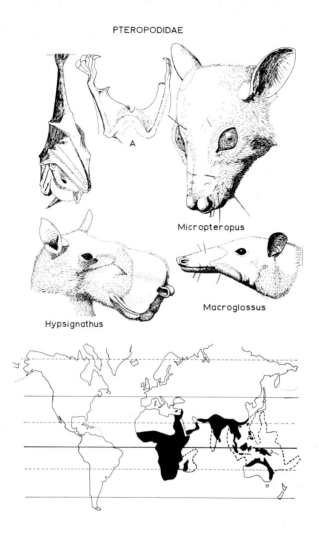

PTEROPODIDAE

A

Micropteropus

Hypsignathus

Macroglossus

Fig 33. Pteropodidae

197

MOUSE-TAILED BATS (fig 34)

Species: 4, all in a single genus, *Rhinopoma*

Recognition: extremely long thread-like tail, almost no tail membrane, long naked snout with upturned tip.

Size: tail about the same length as head and body, usually some 60–70mm; weight about 15–20g.

These are insectivorous bats which live in hot dry areas, seeking shelter in caves, buildings and wells, where they often form small colonies which may have occupied the same sites for hundreds of years. They cling to the walls using all four limbs. At certain seasons large masses of fat form around the posterior part of the body and during cold or very dry weather when food is not readily available the bats are torpid.

The fingers are shorter and the aspect-ratio lower than in most other bats. One species is reported to have an unusual undulating flight pattern, punctuated by long glides.

Postscript: Hill (1974 Bulletin British Museum (Natural History), Zoology *27*) has recently described a completely new family of bats, the Craseonycteridae. *Craseonycteris* is intermediate in character between rhinopomatids and emballonurids, but has no tail at all.

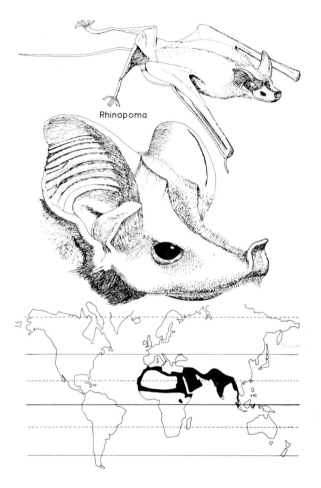

Fig 34.   Rhinopomatidae

SHEATH-TAILED BATS (SAC-WINGED BATS) (fig 35)

Species: 40 in 13 genera.

Major genera (5+ species): *Emballonura, Coleura, Saccopteryx* and *Taphozous*; 6 genera contain only one species each.

Recognition: short tail passes through the membrane and projects from its upper surface. Membrane can slide freely up and down the tail (fig 35A & B) and thus be extended during flight. A tragus is present, but not a noseleaf. Some species have a prominent scent gland in the propatagium, between the shoulder and elbow (fig 35C).

Size: the Emballonuridae are medium-sized bats 35–100mm long, weighing up to about 40g.

One of only 3 bat families with representatives in both hemispheres, but the genera in the Old World (3) differ from those in the New World (10). They are mostly gregarious and feed mainly on insects. At rest some fold the wing-tip upwards on to the dorsal surface of the wing.

Some, like the East African *Taphozous*, are large, fast-flying bats which live colonially in spacious caverns; others like *Rhynchonycteris* and *Saccopteryx* of Southern America are cryptically coloured and roost spaced out on open logs and tree trunks. The ghost bats *Diclidurus* are entirely white, even the wings, though the advantage of this is obscure.

Most emballonurids probably have a clear-cut breeding season, though some *Taphozous* species breed throughout the year.

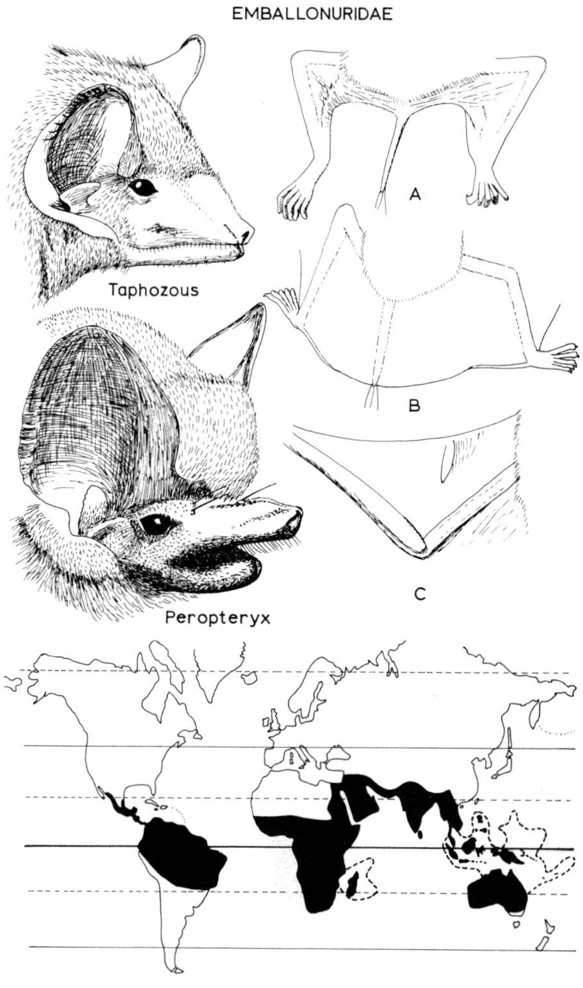

EMBALLONURIDAE

Taphozous

A

B

Peropteryx

C

Fig 35. Emballonuridae

FISHERMAN BATS (fig 36)

Species: 2 in a single genus, *Noctilio*

Recognition: no noseleaf, but the upper lips are thick and heavy and are divided by a vertical fold below the nostrils, producing a heavy-jowled appearance (hence vernacular names 'hare-lip bats' and 'bulldog bats'). The tragus has a serrated posterior margin. The tail penetrates the centre of the uropatagium as in emballonurids. The tail membrane has a very prominent bony calcar stiffening its posterior edge. The feet are very large and armed with huge crescentic claws. Both species have long, narrow wings and very short fur, with an almost hairless abdomen.

Size: these bats weigh up to 70g and are 70 to 140mm long.

Both species are gregarious; *N. leporinus* roosts in caves and rock crevices, *N. labialis*, sometimes called *Dirias labialis*, is more often found in trees and buildings, and feeds on insects.

N. leporinus lives near open water and the coast, flying out at dusk to catch fish, which it gaffs with its claws (it also eats crustaceans and large insects). It swims well, and its short greasy fur does not become waterlogged.

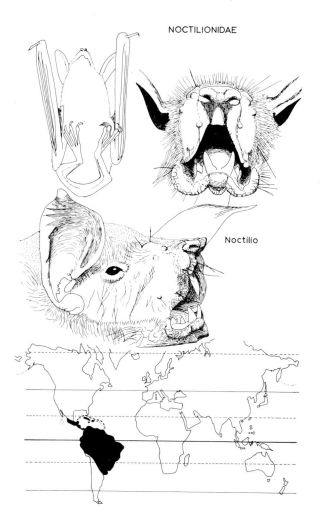

Noctilio

Fig 36.   Noctilionidae

SLIT-FACED BATS (fig 37)

Species: about 10 in a single genus, *Nycteris*

Recognition: nostrils extend posteriorly as a longitudinal groove, ending in a deep pit on the forehead. The fleshy margins of the groove can be opened (fig 37A) or closed (fig 37B). The ears are very long, but the tragus is small. The tail is long and is unique in having a T-shaped end (fig 37C) which serves to support the rear margin of the extensive uropatagium. The fur is characteristically fine and long.

Size: small to medium-sized bats, weighing 10 to 40g, and with a tail approximately the same length as the head and body (45–74mm).

Slit-faced bats usually roost alone or in small groups. They frequently live in very dry areas where they inhabit well-lit but shady places: abandoned wells, hollow trees and shallow caves, and we have found them in very dusty places like old burrows and small holes in the ground; they also have the dubious distinction of inhabiting latrine pits in East Africa. Most species are insectivorous and many take sun spiders and scorpions, presumably caught on the ground.

Nycteris luteola and *N. hispida* are among the few bats which are polyoestrous and conceive a second offspring soon after giving birth to the first, thus producing two litters per year. Nycterid bats are very closely related to the megadermatids, and are included within the latter family by some taxonomists.

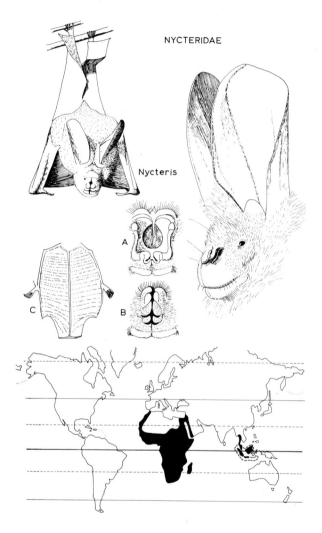

Nycteris

A

B

C

Fig 37. Nycteridae

FALSE VAMPIRES (fig 38)

Species: 5 in 3 genera.

Genera: *Megaderma* (includes *Cardioderma*), *Macroderma* and *Lavia*.

Recognition: big bats with very large ears, joined at the base across the top of the head. Eyes are unusually large for Microchiroptera, and the tragus is bifurcated. A prominent, simple noseleaf extends as a blade-like structure from the nostrils to behind the eyes. No upper incisor teeth. No tail, but the uropatagium has a prominent blood vessel passing down its midline instead. False teats are seen on the lower abdomen, as in Rhinolophidae.

Size: *Macroderma gigas*, the Australian member of this family, grows up to 140mm long (forearm up to 115mm); it is the largest of the Microchiroptera and is among the largest of all bats. The other genera are of more modest proportions, though still over 60mm long.

Unlike true vampires, these bats do not drink blood. *Lavia frons* is insectivorous, but the others also feed on small vertebrates (including fish, frogs, birds and mice), many of them picked off the ground. Low-intensity sonar and large eyes suggest hunting is at least partly guided by sight.

The bats roost singly or in small groups in caves, buildings and hollow trees. *Lavia* is unusual in having yellow wings and often roosts among the twigs of open bushes and trees, where it must remain constantly alert throughout the day.

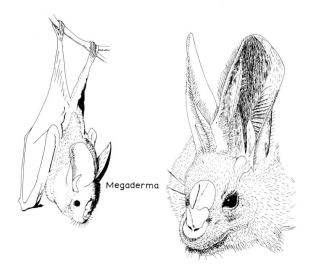

Megaderma

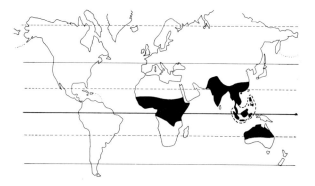

Fig 38. Megadermatidae

207

HORSESHOE BATS (fig 39)

Species: about 50, all but one in the genus *Rhinolophus*.

Genera: *Rhinolophus* and *Rhinomegalophus*.

Recognition: diagnostic, both of family and species, is the complex noseleaf. This has a horseshoe-shaped shallow cone encircling the nostrils and a crumpled triangular leaf (the 'lancet') extending up between the eyes. The third part of this structure, called the sella, is a vertical median partition rising upwards from the base of the lancet and horseshoe. At rest these bats wrap their wings around themselves, rather than hold them folded at each side, giving the appearance of a small dark fruit or a furled umbrella hanging up. There is no tragus in the ear. The tail is relatively short and folded up over the back when at rest.

Size: some horseshoe bats weigh up to 50g; forearm measurements are mostly within the range 30 to 75mm; body lengths range from 35mm to over 110mm.

The complex noseleaf appears to be intimately concerned with the special echolocation system of these bats. Their broad rounded wings produce a distinctive butterfly-like flight pattern. False teats are present on the lower abdomen and are used by the young bats as a point of attachment to their mother in flight.

The temperate species are typically associated with caves, particularly during hibernation when surroundings with a high relative humidity are vital. All are insectivorous.

The genus *Rhinomegalophus* is known from only a single sad-looking specimen from Vietnam and is considered in a recent paper to be a synonym of *Rhinolophus*. Some authors (eg Koopman, 1970) include the family Hipposideridae in the Rhinolophidae.

RHINOLOPHIDAE

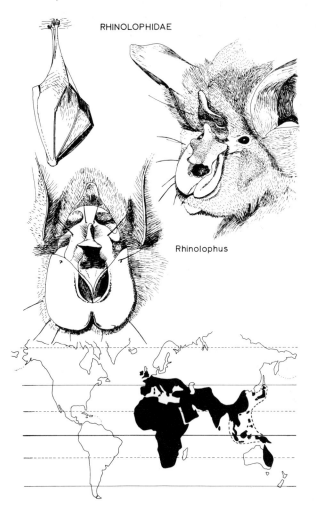

Rhinolophus

Fig 39. Rhinolophidae

LEAF-NOSED BATS (fig 40)

Species: about 40 in 9 genera.

Major genera (5+ species): *Hipposideros, Triaenops*.

Recognition: a noseleaf is present, similar to rhinolophids' but simpler: the horseshoe surrounds the nostrils, but there is no sella (the vertical median partition). The lancet forming the posterior section of the noseleaf is simple and characteristically square-topped in *Hipposideros*, but may have extra vertical projections (usually 3) as in *Asellia*, or multiple foliose elaborations, eg *Triaenops* and *Anthops*. In rhinolophids the lancet is single-pronged and triangular in shape. Hipposiderids have only 2 bones in all their toes, whereas rhinolophids have 3. The two families also differ in the structure of the shoulder girdle and number of lower premolars, but they are obviously closely related and should perhaps all be regarded as one family. Some hipposiderids have no tail; all lack a tragus.

Size: *Hipposideros gigas* is one of the largest of the Microchiroptera, with a forearm length of 110mm. Other hipposiderids, notably *Asellia* species, are small and delicate.

These bats inhabit buildings and underground cavities. Certain species are solitary, others form large colonies; all are insectivorous and frequently fly close to the ground. Sex dimorphism is pronounced in some types and bright orange-colour variants are common among normally drab species. Indeed this family exhibits a range of colours unusual for bats.

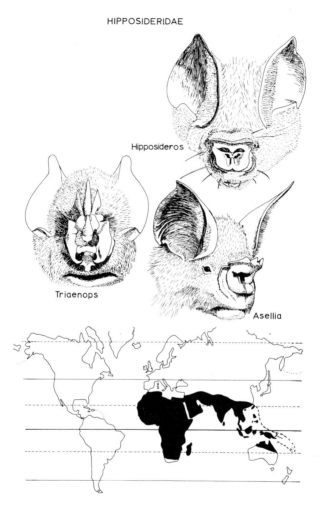

HIPPOSIDERIDAE

Hipposideros

Triaenops

Asellia

Fig 40. Hipposideridae

SPEAR-NOSED BATS (American leaf-nosed bats) (fig 41)
Species: about 140 in 51 genera.
Major genera (8+): *Micronycteris, Artibeus*; 23 genera each contain only a single species; the rest have up to 6 species.
Recognition: the only New World bats possessing a noseleaf, (fig 41A), but this is never so complex as in Old World bats and is absent in some genera (*Chilonycteris, Mormoops, Pteronotus* and *Centurio*), though these often have elaborate fleshy 'chin leaves' instead. All have a tragus.
Size: this large family includes small species and very large ones, from *Glossophaga* (about 45mm long) to *Vampyrum* (c140mm long), the largest bat in the Americas.

An extremely diverse family, forming many evolutionary parallels with quite separate families in the Old World. Clearly defined sub-families include Chilonycterinae, the leaf-chinned bats, which are insectivorous and sufficiently distinct to be regarded by some as a separate family, the Mormoopidae (Vaughan & Bateman, 1970). The sub-family Glossophaginae are long-snouted bats which feed on nectar and pollen and have a very reduced dentition. The rest range from small insectivorous types (*Ametrida*) through the robust frugivorous *Artibeus* and *Sturnira* to the large carnivorous *Phyllostomus* and *Vampyrum*.

Remarkable features are seen: the noseleaf of *Lonchorhina* is as long as its large ears; *Uroderma* and *Vampyrops* have white stripes; the grotesque *Centurio* can pull its 'double chins' up to cover its face; *Tonatia* has been caught in a termite nest and *Artibeus cinereus* folds leaves to provide shelter at its roosting place.

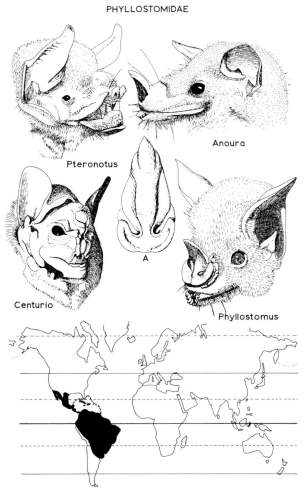

Fig 41.   Phyllostomidae

213

VAMPIRES (fig 42)

Species: 3 in separate genera.

Genera: *Desmodus, Diaemus* and *Diphylla*.

Recognition: a naked U-shaped pad at the end of the muzzle gives a snub-nosed appearance. There is no free noseleaf. A tragus is present and the ears are short. There is no tail and the uropatagium is very small. The molar teeth are reduced but the incisors are large, sharp and directed forwards. In life a vampire scurries and hops about on the ground with great agility; it can raise the body high on its wrists and feet, looking like a giant spider (42A), and can jump backwards to take off (fig 42B & C).

Size: much smaller than their reputation—60 to 100mm long and weighing up to 50g. All 3 genera are similar in size.

Vampires prefer to roost in total darkness, usually in caves and mines, forming colonies numbering anything from one to many thousands. They are shy and usually only emerge on very dark nights. Their echolocation pulses are faint and they fly slowly, close to the ground, in search of a sleeping animal to bite and then lap up the flowing blood.

Desmodus rotundus is the common vampire; *Diaemus youngi* and *Diphylla ecaudata* are less abundant and seem to prefer feeding on birds. The former has white wingtips, the latter is distinguished by having 26 teeth (4 more than the other genera) of which the outer lower incisor has a unique 7-lobed fan shape. Some authors consider vampires to be a sub-family of the Phyllostomidae. They are certainly closely related and seem to have more in common with most phyllostomids than do the Chilonycterinae (Gerber & Leone, 1971).

DESMODONTIDAE

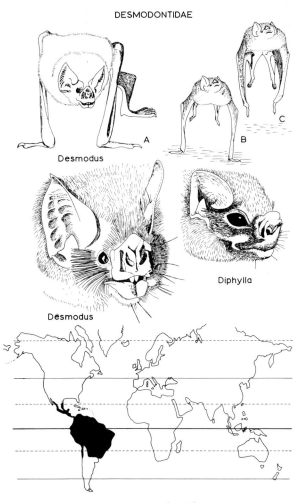

Fig 42. Desmodontidae

215

FUNNEL-EARED BATS (fig 43)

Species: 6, all in the genus *Natalus*.

Recognition: slender, delicate bats, whose very long legs and tail are longer than the head and body. They have large, well separated funnel-shaped ears and a simple muzzle lacking a noseleaf. The eyes are tiny and hidden by fur and hairs on the face. The body fur is long, soft and usually yellow in colour.

Size: small bats weighing less than 10g and only 35–55mm long.

These bats are close relatives of the Furipteridae and Thyropteridae, other relatively insignificant families found in similar tropical lowland habitats. They have a fluttering flight and usually choose to roost only in the darkest recesses of caves and mines. Natalids are insectivorous, taking only very tiny prey; a habit perhaps correlated with the unusually high frequency (up to 170kHz) of their ultrasonic emissions.

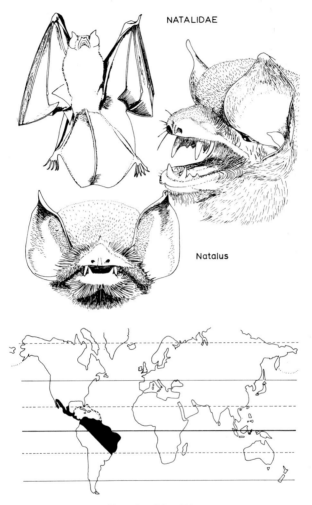

NATALIDAE

Natalus

Fig 43.   Natalidae

SMOKY BATS (fig 44)

Species: 2 in separate genera.

Genera: *Furipterus* and *Amorphochilus*.

Recognition: the thumb is rudimentary, enclosed by the wing membrane and only recognisable externally by the presence of its small functionless claw (fig 44A). The head has a high, domed appearance and the snout ends abruptly in a flat pad. The long tail does not reach the edge of the tail membrane or penetrate its surface.

Size: very small, less than 60mm long and weighing only 5g or so.

These small bats resemble natalids, especially in their big funnel-shaped ears and their occurrence in tropical lowland habitats. They have been collected only rarely, few museums have specimens and virtually nothing is known of their habits or ecology, though their dentition suggests that they are insectivorous.

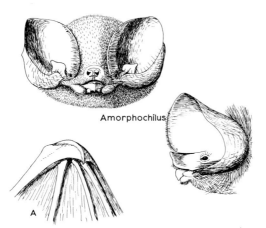

Amorphochilus

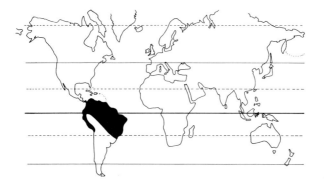

A

Furipterus

Fig 44.   Furipteridae

219

DISC-WINGED BATS (fig 45)

Species: 2, both in the genus *Thyroptera*.

Recognition: small; stalked suckers are present on the wrists (fig 45A) and ankles (fig 45B). Otherwise, with their big funnel ears and high crowned head, they resemble furipterids, except that they have a well-formed thumb and the tail projects a short way beyond the trailing edge of the uropatagium.

Size: small, weighing about 5g. They are 35 to 50mm long, with a forearm length of 27 to 38mm.

The strange discs have a sticky secretion and muscles which enable them to function as genuine suckers: a single one can support the entire weight of the bat as it hangs from a smooth surface. Thyropterids are unusual in that they rest in a head-upwards position, usually beside a curled leaf among the tropical forest trees where they live. They are insectivorous and closely related to the furipterids and natalids; all three, relatively trivial, families probably constitute an offshoot of the Vespertilionidae.

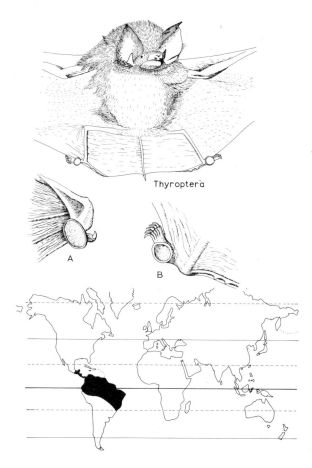

Fig 45. Thyropteridae

SUCKER-FOOTED BATS (fig 46)

Species: 1, *Myzopoda aurita*; confined to Madagascar.

Recognition: sucker discs are present on the wrists (fig 46A) and ankles, but they are not on stalks as in thyropterids and the thumb is reduced to a small vestige. *Myzopoda* has very long slender ears, whose anterior margin is fused to the tragus. A curious mushroom-shaped structure, developed from the hind edge of the pinna, partially blocks the ear aperture (fig 46B). The tail extends well beyond the edge of the uropatagium.

Size: about 55–6mm long, forearm about the same length as the tail—about 47mm.

Myzopoda has rarely been seen or collected and nothing is known of its natural history, though the teeth suggest an insect diet. It is remarkable that suckers should be found in two obscure families in similar habitats but on opposite sides of the world. The suckers and certain skeletal features suggest that *Myzopoda* is a relative of *Thyroptera*. If so, it is difficult to explain their complete isolation from each other; *Myzopoda* is the only bat confined to Madagascar (though it is known from Miocene fossils in Kenya). It is also extraordinary that such peculiar structures as the suckers should have evolved independently, but they are also found (though less well developed) in several genera of vespertilionid bats.

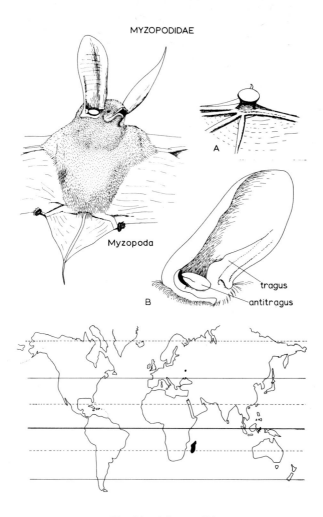

MYZOPODIDAE

Myzopoda

A

B

tragus

antitragus

Fig 46. Myzopodidae

223

VESPERTILIONID BATS (fig 47)

Species: about 275 in 38 genera.

Major genera (over 20 species): *Myotis, Pipistrellus, Eptesicus*: 21 genera contain 3 species or less.

Recognition: this family is so large and diverse that there are few diagnostic features both unique to the family and common to all its members. All except 2 Australasian genera have a simple muzzle with no noseleaf (in these exceptions, about 8 species, the noseleaf is very small): Tragus and tail are present in all genera. The skeleton shows diagnostic specialisations, especially in the shoulder region (cf p 36). Perhaps the best generalisation is that Vespertilionids are those bats which, externally at least, lack the special characters of other families.

Size: sizes span a considerable range, from 30 to 130mm long and 4 to 80g in weight. Measurements are important in separating species, but are too diverse to be diagnostic of the family.

The most widespread family of bats, with representatives in all continents, except in the polar regions. Vespertilionids have succeeded in colonising many remote islands (see dotted lines of fig 47, map) and are often the only bats present. *Myotis* is the largest bat genus (about 60 species) and has a wider distribution than any other mammalian genus, except perhaps *Homo*.

Most vespertilionids are associated with caves, though some species are rarely, if ever, found in them; most are insectivorous, though some are carnivorous and even piscivorous. Some are solitary, others form large aggregations which may split up to form maternity colonies in summer.

Ultrasonic echolocation sounds are usually emitted through the mouth. These are of very low intensity in certain genera, like *Plecotus*, which have enormous ears.

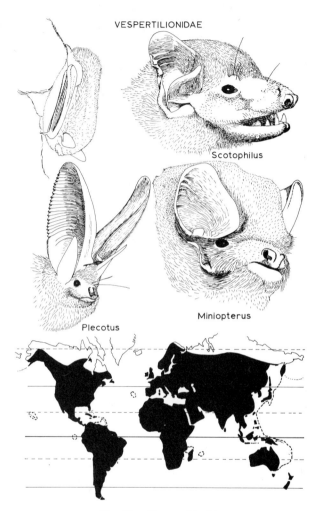

VESPERTILIONIDAE

Scotophilus

Plecotus

Miniopterus

Fig 47. Vespertilionidae

SHORT-TAILED BATS (fig 48)

Species: 1, *Mystacina tuberculata* from New Zealand.

Recognition: the tail projects through the centre of the tail membrane (fig 48A) as in emballonurids. The wing and tail membranes close to the body are thick and leathery and cover the folded wings when at rest. Uniquely, the claws on the thumb and toes (fig 48B & C) have an extra talon on the curved lower side and the bristles on the snout have spoon-shaped ends. The toes of the hind feet are of different lengths (they are usually the same lengths in bats that hang upside-down).

Size: *Mystacina* is about 60mm long with a forearm length of 43mm and a weight of about 20g.

The furled wings, protected by their leathery cover, can be used as forelimbs and enable the bat to scurry about on rocks and trees with great agility. *Mystacina* is a forest-dwelling insectivorous species. It and the vespertilionid *Chalinolobus tuberculatus* are the only bats in New Zealand and the only mammals found in that country which were not introduced by man. Since *Mystacina* has evolved into a form unlike any other bat, its isolation in New Zealand must have occurred a long time ago. This genus has been called *Mystacops* (and the family Mystacopidae) by some authors, including Allen (1939).

MYSTACINIDAE

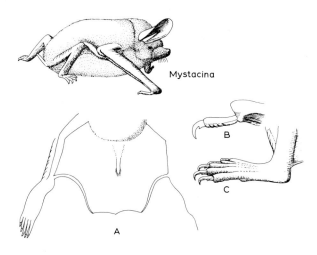

Mystacina

A

B

C

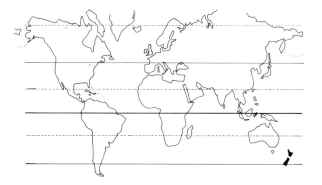

Fig 48.   Mystacinidae

227

FREE-TAILED BATS (fig 49)

Species: about 80 in 12 genera.

Major genera (8 + species): *Tadarida, Molossus, Eumops*.

Recognition: the stout tail projects well beyond the narrow uropatagium so that there appears to be no tail membrane at all, just a free tail. The angular, heavy-jowled face suggests the other vernacular family name of 'mastiff' bats. The ears are usually short, rounded and rather thick, and in most species are joined across the top of the head. The wings are long and narrow. A small tragus is present, but no noseleaf.

Size: another family with a large size-range; measurements are unlikely to aid recognition of the family, though are vital to determine the species. Body lengths are from 40 to 130mm and forearm measurements range from 27 to 85mm.

These insectivorous bats live in warm places, sometimes in vast colonies. They fly straight and very fast and do not flutter about near the ground. They are regarded as the most anatomically advanced bats. Bizarre types include the naked bats *Cheiromeles*, which are nearly hairless, produce a strong smell from special scent glands and have pockets into which they stuff their folded wings when at rest. *Platymops* have a very flat skull enabling them to hide in the smallest rock crevices, *Otomops* are boldly patterned and are the only molossids with very long ears.

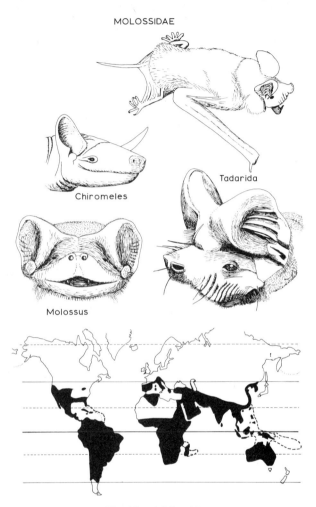

MOLOSSIDAE

Chiromeles

Tadarida

Molossus

Fig 49. Molossidae

BAT GENERA AND FAMILIES

Genus	No of species	Family	Genus	No of species	Family
Acerodon	5	Pterop	Chalinolobus	4	Vesper
Aethalops	2	Pterop	Cheiromeles	2	Moloss
Ametrida	2	Phyllos	Chilonycteris	6	Phyllos
Amorphochilus	1	Fuript	Chiroderma	4	Phyllos
Anamygdon	1	Vesper	Chironax	1	Pterop
Anoura	3	Phyllos	Choeroniscus	4	Phyllos
Anthops	1	Hippos	Choeronycteris	1	Phyllos
Antrozous	3	Vesper	Chrotopterus	1	Phyllos
Ardops	4	Phyllos	Cistugo	2	Vesper
Ariteus	1	Phyllos	Cloeotis	1	Hippos
Artibeus	8	Phyllos	Coelops	3	Hippos
Asellia	1	Hippos	Coleura	5	Emball
Aselliscus	2	Hippos	Cormura	1	Emball
			Corvira	1	Phyllos
Baeodon	1	Vesper	Cynopterus	3	Pterop
Balantiopteryx	3	Emball	Cyttarops	1	Emball
Balionycteris	1	Pterop			
Barbastella	2	Vesper	Depanycteris	1	Emball
Barticonycteris	1	Phyllos	Desmodus	1	Desmodon
Boneia	1	Pterop	Diaemus	1	Desmodon
Brachyphylla	4	Phyllos	Diclidurus	3	Emball
			Diphylla	1	Desmodon
Carollia	4	Phyllos	Dobsonia	9	Pterop
Casinycteris	1	Pterop	Dyacopterus	2	Pterop
Centronycteris	1	Emball			
Centurio	1	Phyllos	Ectophylla	2	Phyllos

230

Bat genera and families

Genus	No of species	Family	Genus	No of species	Family
Eidolon	3	Pterop	Macrotus	3	Phyllos
Emballonura	7	Emball	Megaderma	3	Megader
Enchisthenes	1	Phyllos	Megaerops	2	Pterop
Eomops	1	Mollos	Megaloglossus	1	Pterop
Eonycteris	4	Pterop	Melonycteris	1	Pterop
Epomophorus	8	Pterop	Micronycteris	10	Phyllos
Epomops	3	Pterop	Micropteropus	2	Pterop
Eptesicus	30	Vesper	Mimetillus	1	Vesper
Erophylla	2	Phyllos	Miniopterus	10	Vesper
Euderma	1	Vesper	Mimon	3	Phyllos
Eudiscopus	1	Vesper	Molossops	6	Moloss
Eumops	8	Moloss	Molossus	10	Moloss
			Monophyllus	6	Phyllos
Furipterus	1	Fuript	Mormoops	2	Phyllos
			Murina	10	Vesper
Glauconycteris	6	Vesper	Musonycteris	1	Phyllos
Glischropus	4	Vesper	Myotis	60	Vesper
Glossophaga	3	Phyllos	Mystacina	1	Mystac
			Myzopoda	1	Myzop
Haplonycteris	1	Pterop			
Harpiocephalus	1	Vesper	Nanonycteris	1	Pterop
Harpyonycteris	1	Pterop	Natalus	6	Natal
Hesperoptenus	4	Vesper	Neoplatymops	1	Moloss
Hipposideros	25	Hippos	Neopteryx	1	Pterop
Histiotus	4	Vesper	Nesonycteris	1	Pterop
Hylonycteris	1	Phyllos	Noctilio	2	Noctil
Hypsignathus	1	Pterop	Notopteris	1	Pterop
			Nyctalus	6	Vesper
Kerivoula	15	Vesper	Nycteris	10	Nycter
			Nycticeius	14	Vesper
Laephotis	1	Vesper	Nyctimene	6	Pterop
Lasionycteris	1	Vesper	Nyctophilus	7	Vesper
Lasiurus	12	Vesper			
Lavia	1	Megader	Otomops	6	Moloss
Leptonycteris	3	Phyllos	Otonycteris	1	Vesper
Lichonycteris	2	Phyllos			
Lionycteris	1	Phyllos	Paracoelops	1	Hippos
Lonchophylla	4	Phyllos	Paranyctimene	1	Pterop
Lonchorhina	1	Phyllos	Penthetor	1	Pterop
			Peronymus	1	Emball
Macroderma	1	Megader	Peropteryx	2	Emball
Macroglossus	3	Pterop	Pharotis	1	Vesper
Macrophyllum	1	Phyllos	Philetor	1	Vesper

231

Bat genera and families

Genus	No of species	Family	Genus	No of species	Family
Phylloderma	1	Phyllos	Scotomanes	2	Vesper
Phyllonycteris	4	Phyllos	Scotonycteris	1	Pterop
Phyllops	3	Phyllos	Scotophilus	10	Vesper
Phyllostomus	4	Phyllos	Sphaerias	1	Pterop
Pipistrellus	40	Vesper	Sphaeronycteris	1	Phyllos
Pizonyx	1	Vesper	Stenoderma	1	Phyllos
Platalina	1	Phyllos	Sturnira	4	Phyllos
Platymops	1	Moloss	Styloctenium	1	Pterop
Plecotus	5	Vesper	Syconycteris	3	Pterop
Plecotes	1	Pterop			
Promops	4	Moloss	Tadarida	35	Moloss
Ptenochirus	1	Pterop	Taphozous	12	Emball
Pteralopex	1	Pterop	Thoopterus	1	Pterop
Pteronotus	2	Phyllos	Thyroptera	2	Thyrop
Pteropus	35	Pterop	Tomopeas	1	Vesper
Pygoderma	1	Phyllos	Tonatia	5	Phyllos
			Trachops	1	Phyllos
Rhinolophus	50	Rhinolo	Triaenops	5	Hippos
Rhinomegalophus	1	Rhinolo	Tylonycteris	3	Vesper
Rhinonicteria	1	Hippos			
Rhinophylla	1	Phyllos	Uroderma	1	Phyllos
Rhinopoma	4	Rhinopom			
Rhinopterus	2	Vesper	Vampyressa	3	Phyllos
Rhogeessa	3	Vesper	Vampyriscus	1	Phyllos
Rhynchonycteris	1	Emball	Vampyrodes	2	Phyllos
Rousettus	11	Pterop	Vampyrops	5	Phyllos
			Vampyrum	1	Phyllos
Saccopteryx	6	Emball	Vespertilio	2	Vesper
Sauromys	1	Moloss			
Scleronycteris	1	Phyllos	Xiphonycteris	1	Moloss

BIBLIOGRAPHY

Though long out of date, Allen's book *Bats* still makes good reading and provides a comprehensive review of chiropteran biology. Among the more recent literature, particularly useful books include Walker's *Mammals of the World* (1968), which gives a picture and account of every mammalian genus. Harrison Matthews' *The Life of Mammals*, Vol 2 (1971) more briefly covers similar ground, though with fewer illustrations. Novick & Leen, *The World of Bats* (1970) features superb photographs, and *About Bats* edited by Slaughter and Walton (1970) is a useful and easily read review. The current 'last word' review is *Biology of Bats* edited by Wimsatt (1970), of which two volumes have so far appeared. This is an important and authoritative source work, but not light reading.

For specialised interest, with particular reference to echolocation, there is Griffin's *Listening in the Dark* (1958). Although Griffin and his students have now rendered parts of the book obsolete it remains a splendid, very readable introduction; made the more fascinating as it gives an inside account of a scientist at work pushing back the frontiers of knowledge in an entirely new field.

Detailed regional bat faunas are not listed here, but for North America there exists an excellent guide, with illustrations and maps for all species (Barbour & Davis, 1969), and Goodwin & Greenhall (1961) provide a fine catalogue of Caribbean bats. Sadly there are no comparable works on the British bat fauna; even Southern's *Handbook of British Mammals* (1964) is now out of print.

With such an apparent wealth of literature, where does our book fit in? It is not original, though we feel that our background and experience have enabled us to attempt a balanced review and perhaps avoid the bias that a specialist might show towards his own particular field of interest. To meet constraints of space and cost, much has had to be omitted; for an exhaustive review of the literature one looks to Wimsatt's volumes. Our book is intended to be a review of the whole field of bat biology, detailed enough to be a useful work of reference, yet neither written nor priced with only the academic specialist in mind. It is meant as a guide to the world's bats; what they look like, what they do and how they do it. More detailed, more expensive works are certainly available: if we have

233

Bibliography

stimulated the reader to borrow or buy them then this book will have been worthwhile.

Anon (1971): Report of the committee of inquiry on rabies. HMSO. Cmnd 4696.

Allen, G. M. (1939): *Bats*. Harvard University Press, Cambridge, Massachusetts (reissued in 1962 as a Dover Paperback).

Barbour, R. W. & Davis, W. H. (1969). *Bats of America*. University Press of Kentucky, Lexington.

Barbour, R. W.; Davis, W. H. & Hassell, M. D. (1966). The need of vision in homing by *Myotis sodalis*. *Journal of Mammalogy*. *47* 356–7.

Beauregard, M. (1969). Bat rabies in Canada. *Canadian Journal of Comparative Medicine*. *33* 220–6

Bezem, J. J. Sluiter, J. W. & Van Heerdt, P. F. (1960). Population statistics of five species of the bat genus *Myotis* and one of the genus *Rhinolophus*, hibernating in the caves of South Limburg. *Archives Néerlandaises de Zoologie*. *13* 511–39.

Bezem, J. J. Sluiter, J. W. & Van Heerdt, P. F. (1964). Some characteristics of the hibernating locations of various species of bats in South Limburg. *Proceedings of the Koninklijke Nederlandse Akademie van Wettenschappen, Amsterdam*. *67* 325–50.

Bradbury, J. W. (1970). Target discrimination by the echolocating bat *Vampyrum spectrum*. *Journal of Experimental Zoology*. *173* 23–46

Bradshaw, G. (1962). Reproductive cycle of the California leaf-nosed bat, *Macrotus californicus*. *Science*. *136* 645

Brosset, A. & Deboutenville, C. D. (1966). Le régime alimentaire du Vespertilion de Daubenton *Myotis daubentonii*. *Mammalia*. *30* 247–51.

Busnel, R. G. (Ed) (1967). *Les systèmes sonars animaux*. (Laboratoire de physiologie accoustique, INRA-CNRZ, Jouy-en-Josas, 78, France.)

Church, J. C. T. & Warren, D. J. (1968). Wound healing in the web membrane of the fruit bat. *British Journal of Surgery*. *55* 26–31.

Cockrum, E. L. (1970). Insecticides and guano bats. *Ecology*. *51* 761–2.

Constantine, D. G. (1967a). Activity patterns of the Mexican free-tailed bat. *University of New Mexico Publication*. *7* 1–79.

Constantine, D. G. (1967b). Rabies transmission by air in bat caves. *US Public Health Service Publication no 1617*.

Constantine, D. G. (1970). Bats in relation to the health, welfare and economy of man. In Wimsatt (1970) *The Biology of Bats*. 3 19–449.

Bibliography

Cranbrook, Earl of, & Barrett, H. G. (1965). Observations on noctule bats (*Nyctalus noctula*) captured while feeding. *Proceedings of the Zoological Society of London.* 144 1–24.

Daan, S. (1973). Activity during natural hibernation in three species of vespertilionid bats. *Netherlands Journal of Zoology.* 23 1–71.

Davis, R. (1966). Homing performance & homing ability in bats. *Ecological Monographs.* 36 201–37.

Davis, R. & Cockrum, E. L. (1964). Experimentally determined weight-lifting capacity of five species of western bats. *Journal of Mammalogy.* 45 643–4.

Davis, R. & Doster, S. E. (1972). Wing repair in pallid bats. *Journal of Mammalogy.* 53 377–8.

Davis, R. B., Herreid, C. F. & Short, H. L. (1962). Mexican free-tailed bats in Texas. *Ecological Monographs.* 32 311–46.

Davis, W. H. (1964). Winter awakening patterns in the bats *Myotis lucifugus* & *Pipistrellus subflavus*. *Journal of Mammalogy.* 45 645–7.

Davis, W. H. (1966). Population dynamics of the bat *Pipistrellus subflavus*. *Journal of Mammalogy.* 47 383–96.

Davis, W. H. (1970). Hibernation: ecology and physiological ecology. In Wimsatt (1970), Vol 1.

Davis, W. H. & Hitchcock, H. B. (1965). Biology and migration of the bat *Myotis lucifugus* in New England. *Journal of Mammalogy.* 46 296–313.

Dwyer, P. D. (1970). Social organisation in the bat *Myotis adversus*. *Science.* 168 1,006–8.

Farney, J. & Fleharty, E. D. (1969). Aspect-ratio, loading, wing-span and membrane areas of bats. *Journal of Mammalogy.* 50 362–7.

Fenton, M. B. (1970). A technique for monitoring bat activity with results obtained from different environments in Ontario. *Canadian Journal of Zoology.* 48 847–51.

Fleming, T. H. (1971). *Artibeus jamaicensis*: delayed embryonic development in a neotropical bat. *Science.* 171 402–4.

Gerber, J. D. & Leone, C. A. (1971). Immunologic comparisons of the sera of certain Phyllostomid bats. *Systematic Zoology.* 20 160–6.

Goodwin, G. G. & Greenhall, A. M. (1961). A review of the bats of Trinidad and Tobago. *Bulletin of the American Museum of Natural History.* 122 187–301.

Gould, E. (1955). The feeding efficiency of insectivorous bats. *Journal of Mammalogy.* 36 399–407.

Green, J. H. (1969). *An introduction to human physiology.* 2nd edition. Oxford University Press.

Greenewalt, C. H. (1962). Dimensional relationships for flying animals.

Bibliography

Smithsonian Miscellaneous Collections. 144 1–46.

Greenhall, A. M. (1963). Use of mist nets & strychnine for vampire control in Trinidad. *Journal of Mammalogy. 44* 396–9.

Griffin, D. R. (1958). *Listening in the dark.* Yale University Press, New Haven, Connecticut.

Griffin, D. R. (1960). *Echoes of bats and men.* Heinemann.

Griffin, D. R. & Hitchcock, H. B. (1965). Probable 24-year longevity records for *Myotis lucifugus. Journal of Mammalogy. 46* 332.

Griffin, D. R., Friend, J. H. & Webster, F. A. (1965). Target discrimination by the echolocation of bats. *Journal of Experimental Zoology. 158* 155–68.

Griffin, D. R., Webster, F. A. & Michael, C. R. (1960). The echolocation of flying insects by bats. *Animal Behaviour. 8* 141–54.

Hamilton, R. B. & Stalling, D. T. (1972). *Lasiurus borealis* with five young. *Journal of Mammalogy. 53* 190.

Hamilton, W. J. jnr (1933). The insect food of the big brown bat. *Journal of Mammalogy. 14* 155–6.

Harmata, J. (1969). The thermopreferendum of some species of bats (Chiroptera). *Acta Theriologica. 14* 49–62.

Harrison Matthews, L. (1971). *The Life of Mammals* (Vol 2). Weidenfeld & Nicolson.

Hayward, B. & Davis, R. (1964). Flight speeds in western bats. *Journal of Mammalogy. 45* 236–42.

Heerdt, P. F. van, & Sluiter, J. W. (1965). Notes on the distribution and behaviour of the noctule bat (*Nyctalus noctula*) in the Netherlands. *Mammalia. 29* 463–77.

Henson, O. W. (1967). The perception and analysis of biosonar signals by bats. In Busnel, 1967.

Henson, O. W. jr (1970). The ear and audition. In Wimsatt 1970, 181–263.

Herreid, C. F. II (1964). Bat longevity & metabolic rate. *Experimental Gerontology. 1* 1–9.

Herreid, C. F. (1967). Temperature regulation, temperature preference and tolerance, and metabolism of young and adult free-tailed bats. *Physiological Zoology. 40* 1–22.

Hock, R. J. (1951). The metabolic rates and body temperatures of bats. *Biological Bulletin. 101* 289–99.

Hooper, J. H. D. (1966). The ultrasonic 'voices' of bats. *New Scientist. 29* 496–7.

Hooper, J. H. D. (1969a). Potential use of a portable ultrasonic receiver for the field identification of flying bats. *Ultrasonics. 7* 177–81.

236

Bibliography

Hooper, J. H. D. (1969b). Recording the ultrasounds of bats. *Recorded Sound. 34* 450–5.

Hooper, J. H. D. & Hooper, W. M. (1956). Habits & movements of cave-dwelling bats in Devonshire. *Proceedings of the Zoological Society of London. 127* 1–26.

Hooper, J. H. D. & Hooper, W. M. (1967). Longevity of Rhinolophid Bats in Britain. *Nature. 216* 1135–6.

Jefferies, D. J. (1972). Organochlorine insecticide residues in British bats and their significance. *Journal of Zoology. 166* 245–64.

Jepsen, G. L. (1970). Bat origins and evolution. In Wimsatt (1970) Vol 1 1–64.

Kay, L. (1967). Enhanced environmental sensing by ultrasonic waves. In Busnel, 1967.

Kleiman, D. G. (1969). Maternal care, growth rate & development in the Noctule (*Nyctalus noctula*), Pipistrelle (*Pipistrellus pipistrellus*) and Serotine (*Eptesicus serotinus*) bats. *Journal of Zoology. 157* 187–211.

Kleiman, D. G. & Racey, P. A. (1969). Observations on noctule bats (*Nyctalus noctula*) breeding in captivity. *Lynx. 10* 65–77.

Koopman, K. F. (1970). Zoogeography of bats. In Slaughter and Walton (1970). 29–50.

Koopman, K. F. & Knox-James, J. (1970). Classification of bats. In Slaughter & Walton (1970).

Krzanowski, A. (1961). Weight dynamics of bats wintering in the cave at Pulawy (Poland). *Acta Theriologica. 4* 249–64.

Laidlow, G. W. J. & Fenton, M. B. (1971). Control of nursery colony populations of bats by artificial light. *Journal of Wildlife Management. 35* 843–6.

Leitner, P. & Nelson, J. E. (1967). Body temperature, oxygen consumption and heart rate in the Australian false vampire bat, *Macroderma gigas. Comparative Biochemistry and Physiology. 21* 65–74.

Linhart, S. B. (1971). A partial bibliography of the vampire bats (*Desmodus, Diphylla & Diaemus*). US Dept of the Interior, Bureau of Sport, Fisheries and Wildlife.

Luckens, M. M. & Davis, W. H. (1965). Toxicity of dieldrin and endrin to bats. *Nature. 207* 879–80.

Lyman, C. P. (1970). Thermoregulation and metabolism in bats. In Wimsatt (1970), vol 1 301–30.

Lyman, C. P. & Chatfield, P. O. (1950). Mechanisms of arousal in the hibernating hamster. *Journal of Experimental Zoology. 114* 491–512.

McNab, B. K. (1969). The economics of temperature regulation in neotropical bats. *Comparative Biochemistry & Physiology. 31* 227–68.

Bibliography

McNab, B. K. (1971). The structure of tropical bat faunas. *Ecology. 52* 352–8.

Mejsnar, J. & Jansky, L. (1970). Shivering and non-shivering thermogenesis in the bat (*Myotis myotis* Borkh) during arousal from hibernation. *Canadian Journal of Physiology & Pharmacology. 48* 102–6.

Menaker, M. (1959). Endogenous rhythms of body temperature in hibernating bats. *Nature. 184* 1,251–2.

Menaker, M. (1962). Hibernation—hypothermia: an annual cycle of response to low temperature in the bat *Myotis lucifugus. Journal of Cellular & Comparative Physiology. 59* 163–74.

Möhres, F. P. (1967). Ultrasonic orientation in megadermatid bats. In Busnel, 1967.

Mutere, F. A. (1967). The breeding biology of equatorial vertebrates: reproduction in the fruit bat, *Eidolon helvum*, at latitude 0° 20′ N. *Journal of Zoology. 153* 153–61.

Myers, R. F. (1960). *Lasiurus* from Missouri caves. *Journal of Mammalogy. 41* 114–17.

Nelson, J. E. (1965). Behaviour of Australian Pteropodidae (Megachiroptera). *Animal Behaviour. 13* 544–57.

Neuweiler, G. (1970). Neurophysiologische Untersuchungen zum Echo ortungsystem der Grossen Aufeisennase, *Rhinolophus ferrumequinum*, Schreber 1774. *Zeitschrift für vergleichende Physiologie. 67* 273–306.

Norberg, U. M. (1970). Functional osteology and myology of the wing of *Plecotus auritus* Linnaeus (Chiroptera). *Arkiv für zoologi. 22* 483–543.

Norberg, U. M. (1972). Bat wing structures important for aerodynamics and rigidity (Mammalia, Chiroptera). *Zeitschrift für morphologie der tiere. 73* 45–61.

Novick, A. (1963). Orientation in neotropical bats. II Phyllostomatidae and Desmodontidae. *Journal of Mammalogy. 44* 44–56.

Novick, A. & Griffin, D. R. (1961). Laryngeal mechanisms in bats for the production of orientation sounds. *Journal of Experimental Zoology. 148* 125–45.

Novick, A. & Leen, N. (1970). *The world of bats.* Holt, Rinehart, New York.

Nyholm, E. S. (1965). Zur Okologie von *Myotis mystacinus* (Leisl.) und *M. daubentoni* (Leisl.) (Chiroptera). *Annales Zoologici Fennici. 2* 77–123.

Patterson, A. & Hardin, J. (1969). Flightspeeds of five species of vespertilionid bats. *Journal of Mammalogy. 50* 152–3.

Pennycuick, C. J. (1971). Gliding flight of the dog-faced bat *Rousettus aegyptiacus* observed in a wind tunnel. *Journal of Experimental Biology. 55* 833–45.

Bibliography

Pennycuick, C. J. (1972). *Animal Flight*. Edward Arnold.

Pierce, G. W. and Griffin, D. R. (1938). Experimental determination of supersonic notes emitted by bats. *Journal of Mammalogy. 19* 454–5.

Pohl, H. (1961). Temperatur regulation und Tages periodik des Stoffwechsels bei Winterschlafern. *Zeitschrift für vergleichende physiologie. 45* 109–53.

Pollack, G., Henson, O. W. & Novick, A. (1972). Cochlear microphonic potentials in the 'pure tone' bat *Chilonycteris parnelli parnelli. Science. 176* 66–8.

Poulton, E. B. (1929). British insectivorous bats and their prey. *Proceedings of the Zoological Society of London*. 277–303.

Racey, P. A. (1969). Diagnosis of pregnancy and experimental extension of gestation in the pipistrelle bat *Pipistrellus pipistrellus. Journal of Reproduction & Fertility. 19* 465–74.

Racey, P. A. (1970). The breeding, care & management of vespertilionid bats in the laboratory. *Laboratory Animals. 4* 171–83.

Racey, P. A. (1972). 'Bats'. In UFAW Handbook on the care and management of laboratory animals, ed UFAW. Edinburgh.

Racey, P. A. (1973). The viability of spermatozoa after prolonged storage by male & female European bats. *Periodicum Biologorum (Zagreb). 75* 201–5.

Racey, P. A. & Potts, D. M. (1970). Relationship between stored spermatozoa and the uterine epithelium in the pipistrelle bat (*Pipistrellus pipistrellus*). *Journal of Reproduction & Fertility. 22* 57–63.

Racey, P. A. & Stebbings, R. E. (1972). Bats in Britain—a status report. *Oryx. 11* 319–27.

Ransome, R. D. (1968). The distribution of the greater horseshoe bat *Rhinolophus ferrumequinum*, during hibernation in relation to environmental factors. *Journal of Zoology. 154* 77–112.

Ransome, R. D. (1971). The effects of ambient temperature on the arousal frequency of the hibernating greater horseshoe bat, *Rhinolophus ferrumequinum*, in relation to site selection and the hibernation state. *Journal of Zoology. 164* 353–71.

Ratcliffe, F. (1932). Notes on the fruit bats (*Pteropus* spp) of Australia. *Journal of Animal Ecology. 1* 32–57.

Rauch, J. C. & Hayward, J. S. (1970). Regional distribution of blood flow in the bat (*Myotis lucifugus*) during arousal from hibernation. *Canadian Journal of Physiology and Pharmacology. 48* 269–73.

Ross, A. (1967). Ecological aspects of the food habits of insectivorous bats. *Proceedings of the Western Foundation of Vertebrate Zoology. 1* 205–63.

Schmidt, U. von, & Manske U. (1973). Die jugendentwicklung der

Bibliography

vampirfledermaus (*Desmodus rotundus*). *Zeitschrift für Saugetierkunde. 38* 14–33.

Schnitzler, H-U. (1967). Discrimination of thin wires by flying horseshoe bats (Rhinolophidae). In Busnel, 1967.

Schnitzler, H-U. (1968). Die Ultraschall-Ortungslaute der Hafeisen-Fledermäuse (Chiroptera—Rhinolophidae) in verschiedenen Orientierungssituationen. *Zeitschrift für vergleichende Physiologie. 57* 376–408.

Slaughter, B. H. & Walton, D. W. (1970). *About bats*. Southern Methodist University Press, Dallas.

Sluiter, J. W. & Van Heerdt, P. F. (1966). Seasonal habits of the noctule bat (*Nyctalus noctula*). *Archives Néerlandaises de Zoologie. 16* 423–39.

Southern, H. N. ed (1964). *The Handbook of British Mammals*. Oxford.

Staines, H. J. (1965). Female red bat carrying four young. *Journal of Mammalogy. 46* 333.

Stebbings, R. E. (1965). Observations during sixteen years on winter roosts of bats in west Suffolk. *Proceedings of the Zoological Society of London. 144* 137–43.

Stebbings, R. E. (1969). Observer influence on bat behaviour. *Lynx. 10* 93–100.

Stebbings, R. E. (1970). A comparative study of *Plecotus auritus* and *P. austriacus* (Chiroptera, Vespertilionidae) inhabiting one roost. *Bijdragen tot de Dierkunde. 40* 91–4.

Strelkov, P. P. (1969). Migratory and stationary bats (Chiroptera) of the European part of the Soviet Union. *Acta Zoologica Cracoviensia. 14* 393–439.

Studier, E. H. (1972). Some physiological properties of the wing membranes of bats. *Journal of Mammalogy. 53* 623–5.

Studier, E. H., Beck, L. R. & Lindeborg, R. G. (1967). Tolerance and initial metabolic response to ammonia in selected bats and rodents. *Journal of Mammalogy. 48* 564–72.

Suthers, R. A. (1965). Acoustic orientation by fish-catching bats. *Journal of Experimental Zoology. 158* 319–47.

Suthers, R. A., Thomas, S. P. & Suthers, B. J. (1972). Respiration, wing beat and ultrasonic pulse emission in an echo-locating bat. *Journal of Experimental Biology. 56* 37–48.

Thomas, S. P. & Suthers, R. A. (1972). The physiology and energetics of bat flight. *Journal of Experimental Biology. 57* 317–35.

Van der Pijl, L. (1957). The dispersal of plants by bats (Chiropterochory). *Acta Botanica Neerlandaises. 6* 291–315.

Vaughan, T. A. (1959). Functional morphology of three bats: *Eumops*,

Bibliography

Myotis, Macrotus. University of Kansas Publications, Museum of Natural History. 12 1–153.

Vaughan, T. A. (1970). Chapters 3, 4 and 5 in Wimsatt (1970) vol 1.

Vaughan, T. A. & Bateman, G. S. (1970). Functional morphology of the forelimb of mormoopid bats. *Journal of Mammalogy. 51* 217–35.

Voute, A. M. (1972). Contribution to the ecology of the pond bat *Myotis dasycneme* (Boie, 1925). PhD Thesis, Utrecht.

Walker, E. P. (1968). *Mammals of the World* (2nd edition) vol 1. Johns Hopkins Press, Baltimore.

Webster, F. A. & Griffin, D. R. (1962). The role of the flight membrane in insect capture by bats. *Animal Behaviour. 10* 332–40.

Williams, C. B. (1939). Analysis of four years captures of insects in a light trap. Part 1. *Transactions of the Royal Entomological Society, 89* 79–132.

Williams, C. B. (1961). Studies on the effect of weather conditions on the activity and abundance of insect populations. *Philosophical Transactions of the Royal Society London, series B. 244* 331–78.

Williams, T. C. & Williams, J. M. (1970). Radio tracking of homing and feeding flights of a neotropical bat, *Phyllostomus hastatus. Animal Behaviour. 18* 302–9.

Wilson, D. E. (1973). Bat faunas: a trophic comparison. *Systematic Zoology. 22* 14–29.

Wimsatt, W. A. (1969). Some interrelations of reproduction and hibernation in mammals. *Symposium of the Society for Experimental Biology. 23* 511–49.

Wimsatt, W. A. (1969). Transient behaviour, nocturnal activity patterns & feeding efficiency of vampire bats (*Desmodus rotundus*) under natural conditions. *Journal of Mammalogy. 50* 233–44.

Wimsatt, W. A. (1970). *Biology of bats*, vols 1 & 2. Academic Press, London & New York.

Wimsatt, W. A. & Guerriere, A. (1962). Observations on the feeding capacities and excretory functions of captive vampire bats. *Journal of Mammalogy. 43* 17–26.

ACKNOWLEDGEMENTS

In preparing a review such as this, the greatest debt is owed to the many people responsible for the original research on which it is based. We cannot thank them individually for their assistance but we hope that by citing references to our major sources of information we have gone some way towards acknowledging the indirect contributions made by the many bat biologists that have preceeded us.

In the preparation of this book we have been considerably aided by R. E. Stebbings, Prof D. Pye and Dr P. A. Racey. We are also grateful to Dr M. J. Burgis for helpful criticism of the manuscript and to Mrs I. B. Morris for typing the endless different versions of it.

We are grateful to these people and to the many others who have fostered our interest in bats, but none should bear the additional responsibility of any shortcomings in our book. For these, hopefully few, we alone are to blame.

INDEX

All genera are listed, with their respective families, on pp 230–2 and unnecessary duplication of this list has been avoided by omitting further reference to it in the index.

Index

Index

Index

246

Index